The Odd 1s Out

The Odd 1s Out

How to Be Cool and Other Things I Definitely Learned from Growing Up

James Rallison

A TarcherPerigee Book

tarcherperigee

An imprint of Penguin Random House LLC
375 Hudson Street
New York, New York 10014

Most TarcherPerigee books are available at special quantity discounts for bulk
purchase for sales promotions, premiums, fund-raising, and educational needs.
Special books or book excerpts also can be created to fit specific needs.
For details, write: SpecialMarkets@penguinrandomhouse.com.

LIBRARY OF CONGRESS CATALOGING-IN-PUBLICATION DATA
Names: Rallison, James, author.
Title: The odd 1s out : how to be cool and other things I definitely learned
from growing up / James Rallison.
Other titles: Odd ones out
Description: New York : TarcherPerigee, 2018. |
Identifiers: LCCN 2018003414 (print) | LCCN 2018006569 (ebook) |
ISBN 9781524705657 (ebook) | ISBN 9780143131809 (paperback)
Subjects: LCSH: Conduct of life. | Self-realization. | Adulthood.
Classification: LCC BJ1589 (ebook) | LCC BJ1589 .R35 2018 (print) |
DDC 818/.602—dc23
LC record available at https://lccn.loc.gov/2018003414

Printed in Canada
10 12 11

Book design by Sabrina Bowers

For my odd family who supplied me with hundreds of stories to monetize.

And a special shout-out to my mom, who read every single one of my scripts and was responsible for birthing me.

This is also dedicated to me. I made the book, so it seems fair.

That's all the dedications.
Read the book now.

Contents

Chapter 1

Why I'm Bad at Art
(and Why Being Bad at Something Shouldn't Stop You)

Everyone starts out as a bad artist. And some people stay that way. Fortunately, others improve. No one likes to hear this, but improvement is mostly the result of several hundreds of hours of practice. If adults told children how much work it takes to become an artist, they would all abandon their dreams and make other plans somewhere in the middle of kindergarten. This is why adults always tell little kids that they're great artists, even if they're actually terrible.

Freg

If you looked at my early drawings, you wouldn't think I would grow up to be an artist. My pictures were never the sort that ended up being proudly displayed on the fridge. Most of the fridge space went to my twin sister, Faith. She was such a natural at drawing that you could actually tell what her pictures were.

One time in an elementary school art class, I painted a beautiful portrait of a person. I don't have the exact copy anymore, but I will try to re-create it here:

If you can't tell, this is what I was going for:

For some reason, though, the teacher didn't understand my artistic vision. When it came time to hang everyone's pictures on the wall, she hung mine upside down.

I don't know about you, but I think this picture makes absolutely no sense upside down.

Faith, on the other hand, showed so much artistic talent that when we were both in third grade, my mom enrolled her in after-school art programs. I wanted to come too, for whatever reason, so my mom signed me up as well. While Faith drew pictures of realistic-looking cats, dogs, and other animals, I drew pictures of Chicken Godzilla.

Look, Chicken Godzilla is as tall as an airplane's flight path and can shoot fire *and* eggs. *That's* art.

After that class ended, I didn't draw very much. The fridge space still belonged to Faith. I don't remember if any of the art teachers at school encouraged me, but if they did, they were probably only being polite.

But then junior high happened, and I drew a comic to impress a girl. She was a fan of *Twilight* and so I made a comic strip about people watching the movie. It wasn't funny and it wasn't well drawn, but it was a milestone.

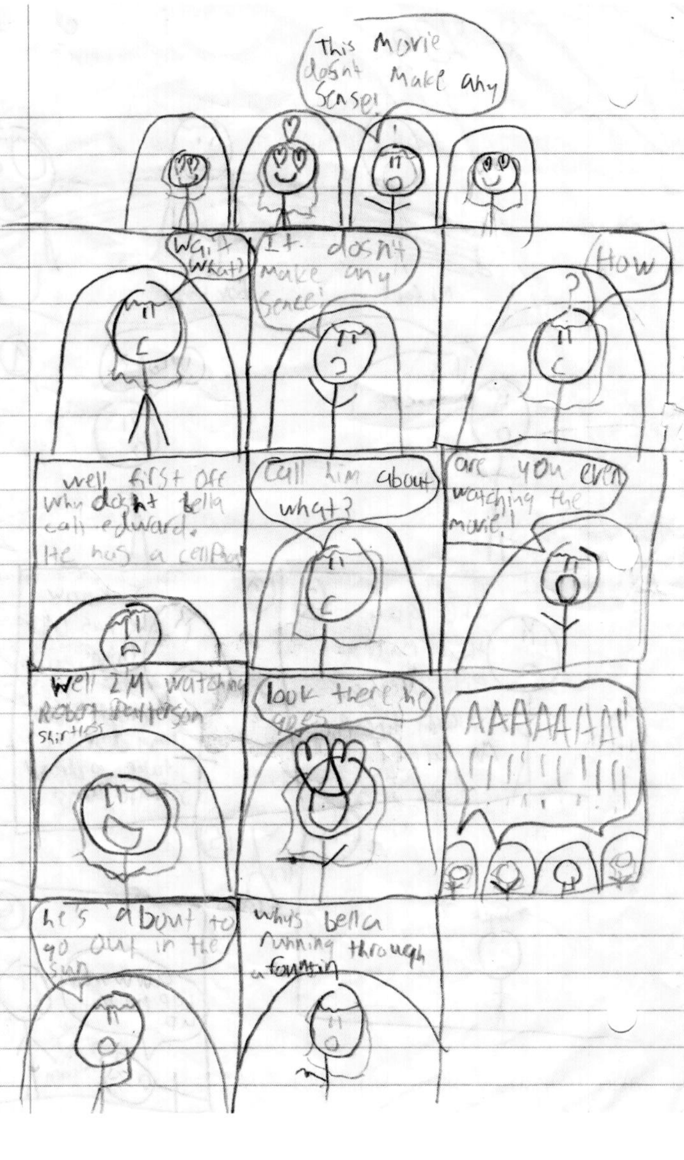
This Movie dosn't Make any Sense!
Wait What?
It dosn't Make any Sence!
How
well first off why doshnt bella call edward. He has a cellPhone
Call him about what?
are you even watching the movie!
Well I M watching Robert Pattenson shirtless
look there he goes
AAAAAAA!!!!!!!
he's about to go out in the sun
whys bella running through a fountin

This isn't the original comic, by the way. I gave that to the girl. I don't know whether she appreciated or kept it, but since I had so much fun drawing the comic, I redrew it and showed it to my friends. I don't know if they appreciated it either, but I decided to keep doing comic strips.

I began drawing six strips a week and passing them around to my friends, who would read them while they were supposed to be listening to our teachers.

My friends loved this pastime. My teachers not so much. I once had a teacher crumple up a page full of my strips because he claimed they were distracting the class. I consider this my first positive review, since it proved that people would rather read my comics than listen to a teacher. (Of course, that contest isn't too hard to win . . .)

At any rate, I became known as the "comic guy," which, relatively speaking, isn't the worst name you can be called in high school.

Eventually I wanted to take my comics to the next level. In fact, I wanted to make them my career. There's never a prouder moment in parents' lives than when their son tells them he wants to be a cartoonist.

They were completely supportive.

Five years later, my hard work is proof that talent is 90 percent determination, 10 percent dumb luck, and 3 percent not paying attention. I kept practicing. And now while Faith draws stunning nature landscapes, I draw pale, bald characters. You'd still probably prefer her art on your fridge, but my drawings are all over the internet. So I guess it all worked out.

Chapter 2

Harry the Moth

My grandmother's nickname for me is Cricket. I don't know how she came up with the name, and it doesn't have anything to do with the next story except that they both deal with bugs.

When you wish upon a star or something...

I'm not really an insect fan. Ladybugs are okay, I guess. (Gentlemanbugs, not so much.) If you asked most people what their favorite bug is, more often than not, they'll tell you that it's butterflies. Which is weird, since butterflies are basically just colorful moths. But for some reason, everybody thinks butterflies are better than moths.

We make children's books about butterflies: We use them as metaphors of change, we go out into fields and frolic around trying to catch them with nets, and some people even collect them. Granted, those people then impale the butterflies onto boards for display, but whatever, it's still a compliment. How many other insects can say they get that much affection? Imagine if we loved cockroaches this much.

Moths, on the other hand, are like the white trash version of butterflies.

Beautiful   Mullet

Even though moths and butterflies are practically the same creatures, we give moths a bad rap. We laugh at them for flying into lightbulbs, even though butterflies would do that too if they weren't asleep at night. Moths are so attracted to bright light that they'll follow one even if it kills them. You might think that this sort of behavior makes them stupid, but I prefer to think it shows how dedicated they can be.

We even get mad at moths for eating our clothes, but if butterflies liked the taste of our clothing, you know they wouldn't hesitate to chomp down on our laundry. Actually, butterflies probably think they're too good for your clothing. They enjoy only the finer things in life, like flowers. You hear that? Butterflies think they're too good for you and your T-shirts.

In Arizona we have your normal, run-of-the-mill moths. You know the type I'm talking about. Small, gray, and they look sort of like somebody's bad paper airplane design. But we also have something called a white-lined sphinx moth. And these moths are like the Godzillas of the moth world.

Actually, I think there is a giant moth in the Godzilla universe. Mothra. This is how much we don't like moths; we turn them into city-destroying monsters. When will the hate end?

I'm sure when they filmed Mothra, they didn't have to use any special effects. They just used a white-lined sphinx moth. Those things could beat up hummingbirds if they wanted.

One night when I was five years old, one of these big boys was chillin' at our porch light. Just hanging out because it loved lights and it was a very dedicated creature. Try finding a butterfly that wants to hang out on your doorstep. Not gonna happen.

Then I guess someone opened the door, and he got inside the house.

More light! This place is absolutely glimmering!

The moth's fate was sealed as soon as it crossed the threshold.

I don't know what the moth did once he was inside our house . . .

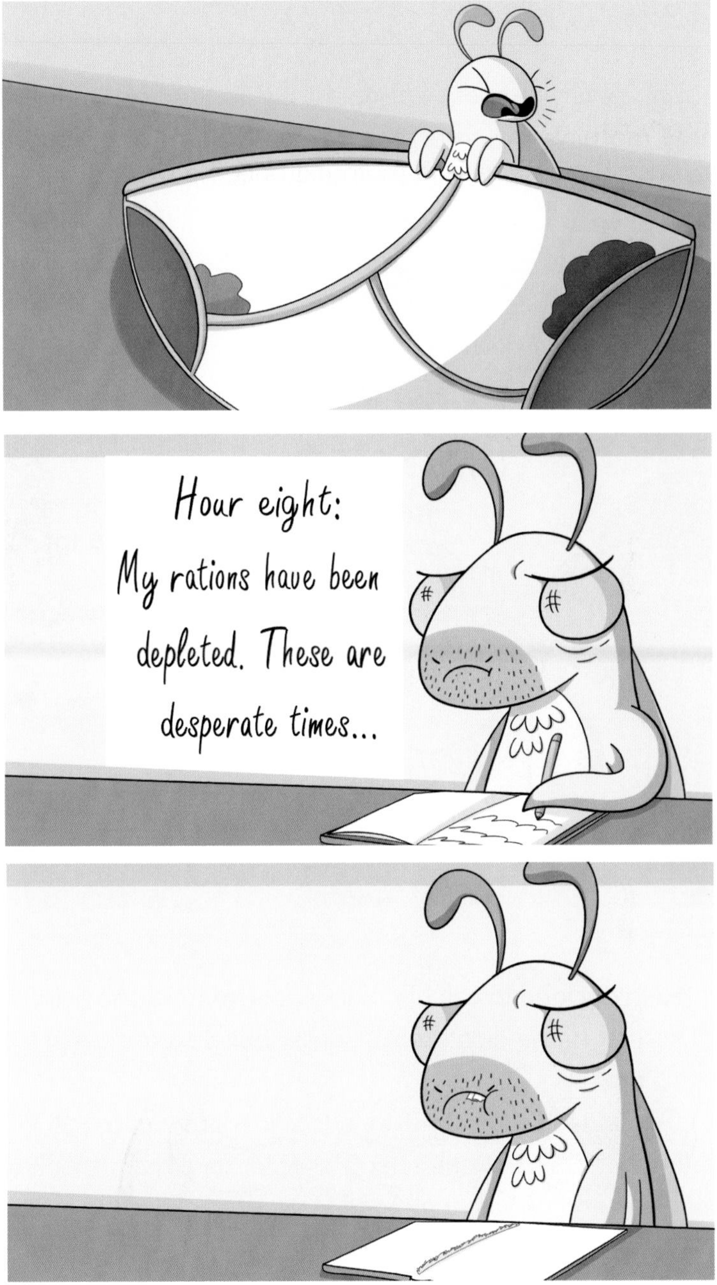
Hour eight:
My rations have been depleted. These are desperate times...

but whatever the moth was doing, it sure tired him out. The next morning my sister and I found him on the kitchen windowsill just lying there—probably thinking about being outside again and trying to escape.

He'd pretty much given up, or maybe he was asleep, because we just scooped him up and put him into a jar, and he became our new pet.

Faith decided to call him Harry. This moth wasn't hairy at all so that name didn't make sense, but we were five, so it didn't have to.

(Around the same time, we adopted a stray calico cat. We called her Calico. Really Harry should have been thankful he didn't end up with the name Moth.)

We put leaves in his jar, which might have been a good idea if he was still a caterpillar, but we were sure we were taking good care of him. We probably should have just fed him T-shirts.

My mom wasn't as thrilled as we were to have a new pet moth.

"I have a good idea," she said. "Why don't you take Harry to kindergarten tomorrow and, I dunno, maybe he can be the class pet there?"

This was back when I thought my mom had good ideas.

So we decided to take Harry to school, because how cool would it be to bring the class a pet you'd captured and en-slaved yourself?

My teacher realized pretty quickly that having a class pet whose lifespan was shorter than the school year wasn't a smart idea. Instead of keeping Harry and studying nature in an educational sort of way, or at least watching him grow lethargic and despondent, drink in hand, watching his stories on the TV,

she decided we could learn about nature by taking Harry out at recess and releasing him. It seemed like a good idea to us, but we were five. This was back when I thought my teacher had good ideas.

A lot of kids' movies have talking animals in them, and usually these animals don't like to be captured. They want to be free and live out in the wild: think *Finding Nemo*, *Spirit*, and *Happy Feet*. It's common knowledge to five-year-olds that every creature walking this earth wants to live in the wild.

The teacher probably suggested releasing him so she wouldn't have to come to school one day and explain to a roomful of horrified five-year-olds why the class pet was lying on its back with his legs stiffly pointing in the air.

(Speaking of setting pets free: My family adopted a lot of stray cats. My mother used to quote the movie *Spirit* as she put them outside at night, and say things like, "Go and run free! Win back your freedom! Don't worry about us; we'll carry on without you!" Unsurprisingly, the cats enjoyed their captivity and always came back in the morning. Probably because of the free food.)

Anyway, we all trooped out during recess, excited to be part of the school's newly instituted catch-and-release moth program. We were like those people who put beached whales back in the ocean, except in this metaphor the whale was already in the ocean minding its own business and two dumb kindergartners shoved it in a fishbowl and moved it miles away from its home.

This was supposed to be a happy kids'-movie moment, seeing the moth get rehabilitated into moth society . . .

But what actually happened was quite different. We gathered around the teacher, she opened the jar, and then she had to shake Harry out of the jar because, well, we've already established that Harry wasn't all that smart.

Eventually, he understood that he was free, that the whole sky was waiting there above him. All that light! He flew upward, wings fluttering, ready to reclaim his moth life.

Well, it turns out there's a good reason giant moths only come out at night, and that's mostly because of camouflage and the fact that their predators are asleep. Harry had neither of those advantages at our playground in the middle of the day.

Not ten seconds went by when a bird from a neighboring tree swooped down and grabbed Harry in its beak. Harry had been a free moth for a good ten seconds before his painful, inevitable death.

Immediately, the entire kindergarten class began screaming. My sister ran after the bird, demanding that he release Harry. Unfortunately, birds don't listen to demands from shrieking five-year-olds. So then the teacher had to give us the talk about how nature is a lot scarier than it's portrayed in the movies.

Basically, the circle of life involves a lot of death.

But on the bright side, we totally made that bird's day.

He was just sitting in a tree, probably wishing Arizona had more worms, and then—boom—free meal. For all we know, that could have been the bird's first time eating a moth. I'm sure that bird told all of his bird friends and they totally didn't believe him. He probably said something like, "Dude, I just caught a moth, like, one of those big ones . . . yeah, in the middle of the day. It was just flying around. No, I'm telling the truth. Dude, there were, like, thirty children who all saw me. Ask any one of them. They'll tell you I caught that moth."

I don't remember what happened for the rest of the day during school, but I'm pretty sure we didn't get much done.

When we got home, my sister tearfully told my mom about how Harry had met his doom. Mom got really "emotional" about it. She said she was trying not to cry, but I'm not so sure about that. I think she was trying not to laugh.

And that's how we scarred our entire kindergarten class.

Like Aesop, I think I should end my stories with morals. So if this story were to have a moral, it would be that sometimes the late bird gets the moth. Also, if you want to have a pet, make sure you get one that's not easily edible.

Chapter 3

How to Be Cool
(in Seventh Grade)

Seventh grade is a time of change. When I say "change," I mean bad things happen to you a lot. If I were to get metaphorical, I'd say seventh grade is that awkward, halfway-in-between time of a frog's life cycle when you've got arm-buds and you haven't lost your tail yet.

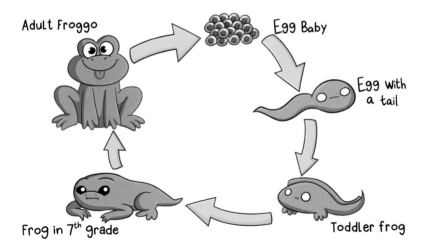

Adult Froggo

Egg Baby

Egg with a tail

Toddler frog

Frog in 7th grade

You're pretty much a mess.

In seventh grade, you're done with elementary school and kid stuff, but you're not anywhere near being an adult. You can't drive anywhere, although there's always that one kid who brags that he can. You have no money. You can't get a job. And you're still living with your parents. Basically, you're a loser.

Elementary school had structure. You had the same teacher and were in class with the same kids all day. You were pretty much forced to be friends with them. Being cool was so much easier. All you had to do was be the fastest runner in your class. Simple.

In junior high, you have to deal with multiple teachers. Just figuring out their quirks, systems, and general neuroses is a job all by itself. And you have different people in most of your classes. So this is also when you get to find out if you have social anxiety or not.

At the beginning of junior high, I was still pretty much in elementary school mode. I just thought about doing things the easiest way possible and didn't care what people thought. I was happy. And clueless.

Like most people, I took PE as an elective class. That was a mistake. I obviously should have taken band. Cool people do band.

In PE, when I wasn't getting hit in the face with a dodge-ball, I was sitting by myself trying to fit in with the other seventh graders.

One day in PE while I was looking at everyone talking to each other and not me, I had a stunning realization.

"Gee willikers, people judge me by the clothes I wear. I know this because *I'm* judging people by the clothes *they* wear."

You never forget the moment when that realization hits you. Hopefully you won't be wearing a stupid T-shirt at the time, like I was. Until then, I had never really considered that *style* was a thing.

I know most everyone picks up on these social clues earlier than I did. If you haven't already picked up on them, I'm really sorry, and also don't worry about picking up on them, because what you wear ultimately doesn't matter. Save yourself; be happy while you still can.

Anyway, up until this point, on PE days, I'd worn my basketball shorts underneath my jeans. That way, no one saw my underwear when I changed. I may not have been cool but I was practical. And self-conscious. Now I finally realized that none of the cool people wore shorts underneath their jeans. Cool people don't care if you see their boxers. At least not in the locker room. (I think they might care in math class, though.)

Now that I've grown up, I've got this cool thing mastered. So sit down, kids. Wait, you're probably already sitting. Well, stop slouching and sit down more seriously because I've been through seventh grade and survived it. I mean, barely, but still. Here are some tips for you to follow so you can be just as cool as me.

Me

1. **Wear low socks.** The lower the cooler. If you're really cool, people shouldn't even be able to tell you're wearing socks. If the only low socks in your house are for the opposite gender, so be it. Be cool and put them on. Your socks may slip down your heels and bunch together in an uncomfortable lump at the bottom of your shoes, but no one said coolness doesn't require sacrifice. When people start to question whether or not you can afford socks, you know you've done it right.

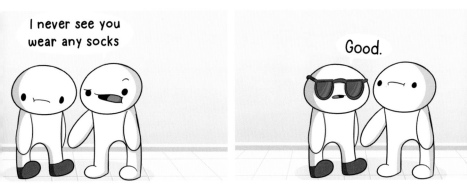

I never see you wear any socks

Good.

2. Wear skinny jeans with holes in them. If you have to pick between skinny jeans and jeans with holes, pick skinny jeans. You can make the holes later. Your jeans should be so tight that you can't bend down. If you need to pick up something on the floor—too bad. That's the level of skinny we're talking about. Be prepared for old, uncool people to frequently make comments to you like "Why do you pay for pants with holes in them?" And "How do you even fit in those jeans?" Ignore these people. When they were in seventh grade, they wore knee socks.

3. **Wear something with a skull on it.** Now some of you might be thinking, "James, all this advice sounds like you're just trying to be edgy." Yeah, well, that was the sort of thing that was cool when I was in seventh grade. Wearing the remains of dead people is a fashion choice. Also, try to listen to songs with depressing, angsty lyrics. Cool doesn't necessarily mean happy. You gave up happiness when you started caring about what other people think.

4. **When heading to the cafeteria for lunch, don't run ahead of everyone to be at the front of the lunch line.** For some reason, cool people don't do this. Personally, I would rather eat first, but whatever. I don't make the rules. Except in this case.

Don't get excited about anything, ever. Cool people are too cool to actually care about things.

5. **Wear a shirt that says, "I'm cool."** This will trick people into thinking you're cool.

Seriously. Just go look around your school and see how many people are wearing designer labels.

• • •

In case you're doubting all my advice, I'll have you know that after months of implementing these exact methods, I finally got noticed.

No, just kidding. That's not what happened. But one of the popular girls came up to me in class and gave me an invitation to her thirteenth birthday party. You may not know this, but turning thirteen is a big deal because it means you're legally a teenager. You finally get to add the word "teen" to the end of your age.

The girl was having a swim party in her backyard. She had a huge house with an amazing pool that ran right up next to a man-made lake. Stray ducks could just glide by you as you swam. That's cool. If you don't have stray ducks in your pool, just give up trying now. You'll never be as cool as this thirteen-year-old girl I knew.

Anyway, going to a pool party meant that not only was I going to be with the popular people, I was going to be *shirtless* with the popular people. It was all part of hanging out with the elite.

Unfortunately, there were three problems with going shirtless:

One, I have an indented chest. I sort of look like someone punched me in between the nipples. It does come in handy when I'm lying down. Then I have a place to put snacks.

Two, I also had stretch marks all across my back from an intense growth spurt. Imagine tiger claw marks but without the good story to explain them. They've faded now, but in seventh grade they were purple.

Three, I didn't have abs. And all seventh graders need to have abs. That's the sign of a cool dude. (Make that my tip number six: Have abs.) So for the week leading up to the party, I did sit-ups in my room every night for as long as I could.

You're probably thinking, "This sounds like something an insecure person would do." Well, yeah. I never said cool people weren't insecure.

I had an idea that would take care of both the stretch marks and the indented chest. I decided to wear a towel hanging over my shoulder that covered my chest and back, sort of like a Greek toga. Then when I got to the party, I would quickly hop in the pool and never get out.

When the big day came, I was ready.

I confidently went to the party and was shown to the pool. All the popular people were there. I knew who they were, although I don't know if they knew who I was. There were also quite a few of the not-so-popular people around the pool. Like, the birthday girl obviously invited a lot of people from our grade. I think she just wanted the presents.

Oddly enough, my twin sister didn't get invited.

So after all of my intense preparation and training, being at the party turned out to be a lot like being at school—except I was shirtless and my stomach hurt from all the sit-ups I'd done.

Some of you reading this book might be in seventh grade or starting seventh grade soon. Maybe you're an adult who still doesn't feel cool. I could say something cheesy like "Be yourself." Or "You'll be fine. It's only seventh grade."

Instead, I'm going to tell you the truth: No matter who you are, you will be awkward in seventh grade. And when you're older, you'll still feel awkward sometimes. There are no real cool people.

You might think, "But I'm pretty mature for my age. I wear skeletons."

No. You're still not cool. Just get through the seventh grade. One day you will morph out of your tadpole-like stage and become a beautiful butterfly. I mean, frog. Whatever. It doesn't matter. You'll be better than a seventh grader.

Chapter 4

Perks of Being the Younger Brother

People have always compared me to my older brother, Luke. It's easy to do, considering we're polar opposites in many ways. He has curly brown hair. I have straight blond hair. Even as a child he was tall and muscular, while I was short and skinny. I wanted to be a cartoonist when I grew up. He wanted to be an assassin. They're both unreasonable dreams, really. (We're, like, 57 percent sure he was joking.)

Even at a preschool age, Luke was much bigger than me. When I was four-years-old, I wore the shoes he'd worn as a two-year-old. And since he was three years older than me, he was always faster, more mature, and better at just about everything. Luke did gymnastics for years and because of that, he was always much stronger than me and anyone I'd ever met. He liked to play rough, push me, pin me to the floor, that sort of stuff.

Based on true events

When I was a freshman in high school, Luke was a senior. At freshman orientation, some of Luke's senior football friends came up to me. (Did I mention that he was also a starting player on the football team? It probably didn't need saying.) One of his friends looked at me and said, "You're not nearly as muscular as Luke."

Some people might have felt bad in that situation, but at that point I was used to feeling bad. I had trained for it all of my life. Without missing a beat, I said,

Because it was true. We can't all be Lukes.

But being a younger brother also has its advantages. Historically, older brothers used to get all the inheritance. Since then, younger brothers have made great strides. Now all older brothers get is the right to be Player 1 in video games. So being an older brother isn't always what it's cracked up to be.

Older siblings are supposed to be the responsible ones, so whenever the two of us would get in trouble, he'd take all the blame.

Luke had a serious sweet tooth. At our house, nothing containing sugar was safe from him. Mom made cookies? Instantly gone. I spent Halloween night going to all the right houses and getting the perfect mix of candy? Gone by morning. My parents hid chocolate chips in the pantry behind cans of green beans, and Luke used his stealthy assassin skills to steal them. My parents finally put a lock on their closet door and hid the key so that they could keep sweets in the house without having them immediately disappear.

One day when I was about seven and Luke was ten, my parents forgot to lock their closet and foolishly left a three-pound bag of Skittles completely unprotected.

For some reason, he believed that he wouldn't get in trouble for eating all the Skittles if nothing remained of the crime. Stealing Logic 101: You have to get rid of the evidence. He knew he wouldn't be able to eat the entire bag while Mom was out, so he enlisted my help.

You know how adults always tell you that if you eat too much candy you'll get sick, but you never do? Well, that's because you've never eaten three pounds of it. Three pounds is how much a small Chihuahua weighs. We ate the equivalent of a Skittle Chihuahua. But we accomplished our goal.

When my mom came home, she was none the wiser. Totally didn't notice the missing Skittles bag or the fact that our tongues were multicolored. Everything would have been fine if I hadn't blown our cover.

You might be expecting me to say that I slipped up and mentioned the candy. But no. I kept the secret. Unfortunately, my stomach didn't. The Skittles wanted to make a reappearance. And they did, when I threw up all over the family room carpet.

The thing about throwing up Skittles is that it's pretty obvious that you ate something rainbow-colored.

I didn't have to fess up. The proof was in the pudding, or in this case, the rainbow-colored throw-up.

For punishment, my mom always handed out extra chores. Luke had to go to the backyard and pull weeds. And I got to lie on my bed and recover. When Luke protested that this wasn't fair, my mom said,

As I said, there are advantages to being the youngest.

But this wasn't the only time I got into trouble with my brother. Remember how I said Luke wanted to be an assassin? I wasn't totally joking. One of the video games he always played was *Prince of Persia*. In the game, the main character does cool parkour. He runs up and across walls, does backflips, and has a dagger that can turn back time. Luke took a lot of inspiration from this character and was determined to try some moves himself. Since he was in gymnastics, he knew what he was doing.

Sort of. He wasn't that good at it. (Sorry if you're reading this, bro.) With one hand on the banister, he tried to run horizontally around our stairwell.

His first step went right through the wall.

No matter how unobservant your parents are, there are some things they are bound to notice. Like foot-sized holes in the stairwell.

Thinking of the simplest solution to avoid a lot of extra chores, I ran up to my room and grabbed a "Keep Calm and Carry On" poster. (Back then it wasn't a dead meme. I thought it was inspirational.)

Before I had a chance to get tape, my mom walked out of her room and began heading down the stairs. I just stood there, holding the poster over the hole, and said,

My mom walked by and said,

and then she just walked away. I'm still dumbfounded to this day at how well my plan worked.

Of course, the poster technique didn't work for long. Mom vetoed our decorating attempts and found the hole.

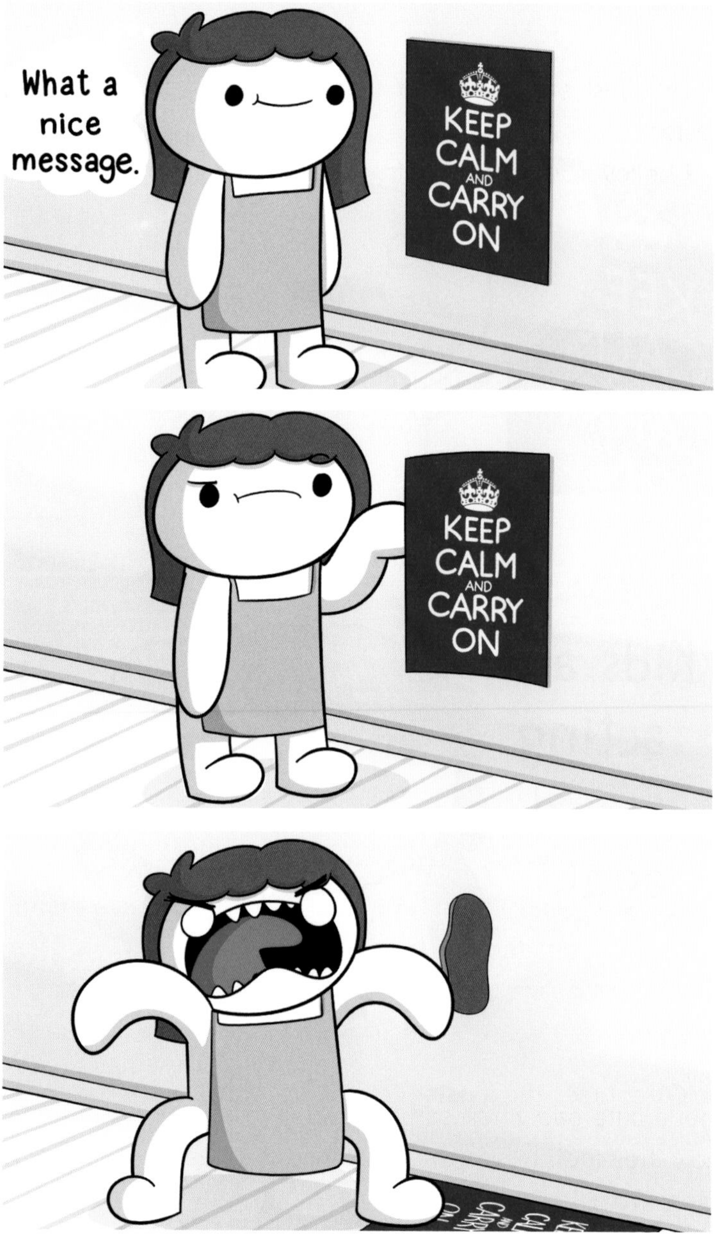
What a nice message.
KEEP CALM AND CARRY ON
KEEP CALM AND CARRY ON

Let's just say she didn't follow the instructions on the poster.

I believe our yard was free of weeds for several weeks afterward.

Besides getting you into trouble, older brothers have other good purposes. Being Luke's younger brother taught me a valuable lesson: It's okay to be number two. It's okay to lose at every video game and board game. As Luke grew more competitive, I became less so. Now that I'm older, if I'm playing a video game with somebody, sometimes I lose on purpose just to make the other person happy. And I always feel a little bad when someone else loses because I know how they feel. I used to experience that feeling every day, repeatedly.

Plus, when you're doing something awkward or cringey, older brothers tell you. Kinda like a bully who also loves you.

I guess at this point, I should mention that I have a little sister, which technically makes me an older brother too. I do my best to fulfill the older brother role and frequently tell her when she's doing something wrong.

In conclusion, older brothers make us who we are today: anxious, traumatized, and slightly neurotic. So thanks, older brothers, you're the best!

Chapter 5

Freshman Year:
Accidentally Dating My Sister (Not Clickbait)

Starting ninth grade is probably the worst decision I've ever made.

Okay, I didn't actually have that much choice in the matter. The educational system made me go to high school. But if I could go back in time and change anything about my life, it would be my entire ninth grade career. High school is such a weird time to be a person.

Luckily, I wasn't that social in high school, which left me plenty of time to draw comics. I went to very few parties and at the ones I did go to we played Magic: The Gathering or watched Disney movies. So, yeah, those parties were always pretty crazy.

High school is nothing like it looks in the movies. No one sings, there's no catchy dance numbers, and in Arizona no one even has lockers. Schools don't trust kids to have lockers. Nope. Too much responsibility. Lockers only lead to trouble.

But I didn't go to a public school in ninth grade. I went to a preparatory school that made us wear uniforms, wake up early, and use lockers. (Responsibility!) Now, don't go thinking that attending preparatory school turned me into some preppy smart person. Maybe the opposite happened.

The school was so small that everyone in the same grade knew each other. For the ninth graders, there were four possible sections to be placed in and everyone in your section had classes together. We didn't switch around like the working-class *public school*. None of that mixing, mingling, and making new friends for us. We had to look at the same faces all day long, all year.

When my twin sister, Faith, and I went to the school with our mom to pick up our schedules, we weren't expecting to be together for every single class—including French, which was a language I didn't even want to learn.

It turns out, our mom requested that we be in the same section. Because apparently, she didn't think we could handle being in high school on our own. Which is strange because Faith and I had only been in the same classes together up until the second grade. After that we split up and would only ever see each other on weekends, like kids in a divorced family who picked different parents. So we were pretty used to not having classes together.

Initially neither of us was happy about being in a section together.

Mom said she could talk to the administration and request that we be split up, and asked which one of us wanted to switch schedules.

Here's the thing, though: Neither of us wanted to be the one to switch. We were too socially anxious and awkward to go through the bother. So in some ways, it's a good thing we had each other. Well played, Mom.

Anyway, that's how we ended up in the same section.

After the shock of having my sister in every single class wore off, I found that there were some advantages to having a more responsible twin in class with me. She could help me with my homework.

She remembered what the lessons were.

And she helped me take tests.

So since Faith and I didn't know anyone, we sat next to each other in all of our classes. As the school year went on, we got to know more people and made new friends. It was a long year of waking up early, writing pages of essays, and having to deal with lockers, but soon it was all going to be over.

Then one day—it was about the second-to-last week of school and classes had just ended—Faith and I were walking back to our lockers. While we went down the hallway, I thought of this random joke. Keep in mind, we were both fourteen, so you know, we were still kind of weird: puberty and stuff. I turned to my sister and said, "Faith, you know what would be funny: if you bump into someone and then say, 'Oh, sorry. I didn't mean to bump into you. Let me apologize with my sympathy rub.'"

And then I proceeded to rub my sister's arm, slowly and gently, because that's what a sympathy rub is.

I mean, it's not my best work, but I still thought it was funny. The joke was that a sympathy rub is weird. I don't think I'd actually ever try it out on anyone to see how effective it was as a form of apology—especially since it ended up getting me in a whole lot of trouble. But who knows? Maybe it could comfort someone someday.

Unfortunately, there was a teacher walking by who didn't appreciate my humor. (This wouldn't be the first or last time.) She was a middle school teacher, so we'd seen her around before, but we'd never talked to her.

She stopped and asked us, "Hey, do you two know the school's policy on public displays of affection?"

My sister responded with, "Yep," and started to walk away.

The teacher said, "Oh, I'm not done."

The lady then began to give us a lecture about why we had to keep our feelings for each other outside of school. She said stuff like, "I know you're both young and in love. But your hormones are all out of whack, and now is not the time to be going steady with someone."

Apparently, this teacher had seen us sit next to each other in classes, walk with each other in the hallway, and work on homework together in the lobby, and naturally assumed that we were madly in love.

Faith and I looked at each other, both thinking, Do we tell her?

You know, looking back, we probably should have stopped her somewhere in the middle of her speech about why we shouldn't be going steady, but we didn't want to make the teacher feel *awkward* or anything. We both had social anxiety, remember? So we just kept our mouths shut and nodded. And I remember while this was happening, my friend Anthony walked by and, knowing we were brother and sister, he was extremely confused about why we were being told not to show our feelings for each other in school.

After the teacher was done talking and had left, I thought the experience was hilarious and wanted to tell everyone in the whole school, but Faith was mortified and wanted to keep it quiet.

Down the hall, Anthony was waiting for us and he asked if we'd gotten called out for PDA. I told him my sympathy rub joke, and Faith made him swear to never tell anyone.

And this would probably be the end of the story, except the next day, while our geometry teacher was going over another section, the teacher that called us out came in and asked the geometry teacher, "Hey, do you know the blond curly-haired girl with the boyfriend that looks just like her?"

I'm sorry, but just saying that sentence probably should have triggered some sort of red flag.

"You mean Faith and James?" my geometry teacher asked.

"Yes," the middle school teacher said. "I saw them holding hands."

Which we *weren't*, by the way. I was giving her a *sympathy rub.*

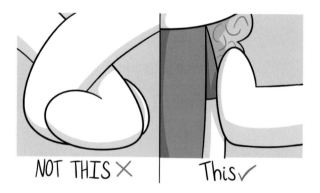

NOT THIS ✕   This ✓

But the entire class burst out laughing anyway. So much for Faith wanting to keep the whole thing a secret.

The geometry teacher broke the news. "They're twins."

So the middle school teacher ended up feeling awkward anyway. I still thought the whole thing was hysterical. And Faith was glad there were only two more weeks of school left.

The lesson here is, if you think speaking up to correct someone might make them feel awkward, you should probably speak up and make them feel awkward anyway. Because if you don't, the whole thing might just become more awkward for everyone. Also, although my studies are inconclusive, sympathy rubs might not be the best form of apology.

Chapter 6

PE

If you grew up in the great American education system, you probably had to take a physical education class to graduate from high school. I actually don't know if it's required everywhere in America, but it is in Arizona. Overall, I'm all in favor of lifting weights and running around for no reason. I understand why schools make kids take PE. (Let's not beat around the bush, it's because we're fat.)

But I think the course could use some changes. Just like with every other class, there should be an honors PE. I'm not saying this because I was a big tough guy who wanted the extra challenge in school. I was just the opposite. Right now, in PE classes you'll have a two-hundred-pound football player, a one-hundred-pound chess club member, and everyone in between all exercising together.

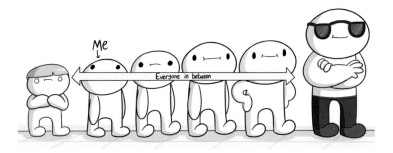

Playing flag football and basketball with a group of testosterone-jacked alpha males is never fun, especially if you're on the "beta" side. And if you haven't figured this out already, I am very, very beta.

I just think I would have enjoyed PE more if all the alpha males were in another section. Although, I guess that's why we have school sports.

Normally to get the PE requirement out of the way, freshman girls at my school took dance and freshman boys took standard physical education. Although, sometimes the really wimpy boys took dance class too. Maybe they were actually the smart ones, because they got to hang around with all the girls. Maybe I should have taken dance.

Since I went to a preparatory school in ninth grade, I took PE my sophomore year, once I was back in public school. It didn't make a difference since I still fit in perfectly fine with the other skinny white boys who weren't smart enough to take dance.

During the first ten minutes of class, we were supposed to get dressed. For guys, getting dressed takes about fifty seconds, so we would just goof off until the coach marched into the locker room and yelled,

Actually, I want to talk about locker rooms for a few paragraphs.

Who decided it was socially acceptable to get completely undressed in front of strangers just because you happen to be standing in a locker room? You would never do this in, say, English class.

Luckily, in high school all we did was take off our pants and put on our gym shorts. We were young and awkward so we all silently agreed that we would just look straight forward, no peeking, and we would all put on our gym shorts without talking. Kinda what we men do when we're at urinals.

Honestly, that's a fine and acceptable thing to do in the locker room. What I have problems with is 100 percent, full-on nudity. In college, I signed up to use the school's gym because I was going to class and drawing all day—meaning I was on my butt a lot and I needed to get my internet-doctor-recommended ten thousand steps in—and I wasn't eating any healthy food.

Anyway, one time at college I was in the locker room putting my clothes back on using the same tactic I did in high school: I wasn't looking around. I was just looking straight ahead. But then someone turned the corner—and I didn't get a good look at him (thankfully), but as he walked past me, in my peripheral vision I thought I saw some cheeks. I turned my head

and he was completely naked!

Aw, James, why don't you act like an adult? You're in college. People have butts, get over it.

Listen, this guy was a complete stranger. For all I know, he could have been in one of my classes (I didn't get a good look at his face, only his butt). I understand that you're supposed to shower in the locker room, but towels exist for a reason. Don't just go flinging your nasties out for everyone to see. Am I making a big deal of this? Because I feel like you're judging me. That wasn't even the only time I saw people walking around naked. It happened quite a bit. That's why I get a locker closest to the door now.

But back to PE: One day while we were waiting for the coach to come in and give us the "Okay, let's do this!" line, we got bored. To entertain ourselves, we took water bottle caps from the trash and started flicking them around like they were little tiny Frisbees.

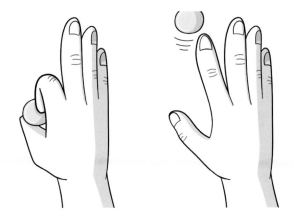

This progressed into shooting caps at each other. I'm pretty sure I was the one who started this trend because, you know, I was the high-and-mighty sophomore in a sea of freshmen. But whatever. Whoever started it, it was all fun and no one got hurt.

In that moment, the jocks and the nerds were all together. We'd bonded over turning lids into weapons.

After the coach came and got us that day, we had an extra hard workout. We ran two laps instead of one. We had to do wall sits while holding medicine balls. And afterward, when we were all sweaty and ready to collapse, the coach said to us, "You know why today was extra hard? It was because you were flicking bottle caps."

How does flicking bottle caps equal fifty minutes of torture? I mean, it was probably healthy for us, but I don't see the correlation.

About a month after the bottle cap incident, these two alpha guys got the idea to play a game called "bodies." If you aren't sure what bodies is, it's a *game* where you punch someone. That's it. That's the entire game. You're not allowed to hit people's faces, though. Just their bodies . . . which is why it's called bodies.

This should be an Olympic sport.

You'd think at least one of us would have said something like, "Hey, you guys, um, Coach didn't like it last time when we were messing around. Uhhhh, maybe we shouldn't do this."

I mean, someone could have gotten hurt.

So, you know, being the older and taller one, I obviously couldn't let that happen. Without watching.

These two kids started playing, and one kid wasn't even punching back, which is a strategy I would *not* recommend while playing this particular game. Maybe the kid thought he was like Harry Houdini. (Short lesson about Harry Houdini: The man thought that his ab muscles were so strong, he told people to punch him and claimed he would absorb the punch.)

(Turns out, this also was not a particularly good strategy, because Houdini ended up dying from a ruptured appendix after someone punched him. How embarrassing.)

Anyway, the dude in my PE class also didn't fare well at this game. He used the Houdini strategy and was taking the punches, then he fell, hit his head on the tile floor, and didn't get up.

Obviously none of us had a medical background, so we just gently slapped the guy a couple of times and said, "Hey, bro, are you gonna wake up, bro?"

That didn't work. So we had to tell the coach, and he went and got the nurse. By the time the coach called the nurse, the kid had woken up a little. He was just being a wussy and not moving. I'm pretty sure he was conscious the whole time.

The coach asked him what happened and the dude *knew* he would get in trouble if he told the truth so he came up with one of the best explanations I've ever heard:

Although, it's possible that he wasn't lying and the head trauma made him legitimately forget.

The coach sent him to the nurse, then turned to the rest of us and asked, "What happened?"

Everyone was, like, "Uh, geez, yeah, uh, he just passed out."

And we *almost* got away with it except this *one kid*—I forget his first name, but his last name was Ferilikins or something—told the coach, "They were playing bodies" and then explained that "Person A punched Person B" (not his exact words).

Thanks, Ferilikins.

Fortunately, right then the nurse called the coach and said that the kid was going home and needed his clothes. So the coach told us, "I need someone to bring his stuff to the health office."

I yelled,

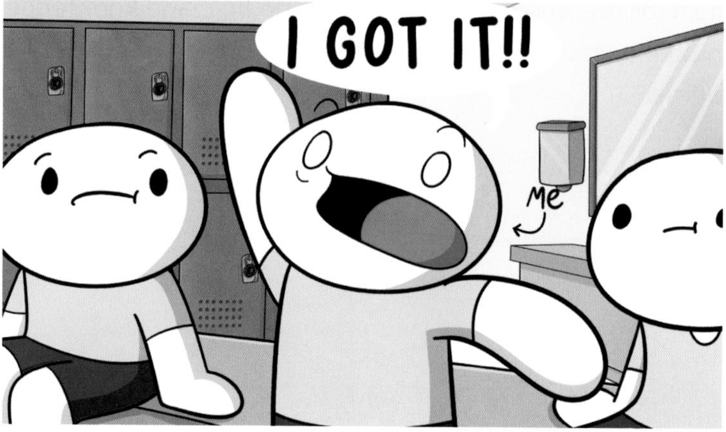
I GOT IT!!
Me

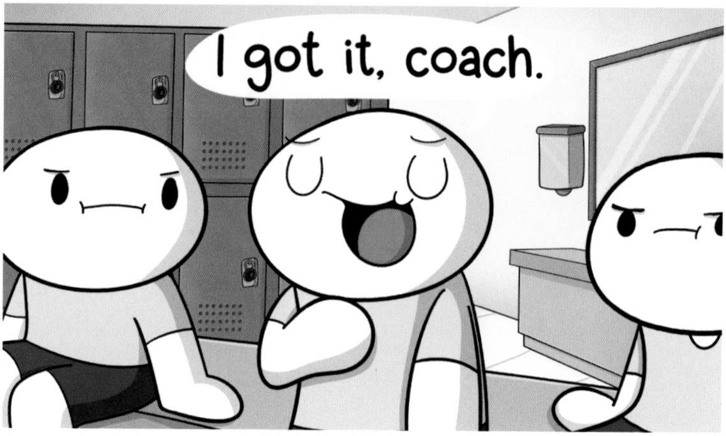
I got it, coach.

"Don't worry, I'll get his clothes."

I'm *told* that the class had to do lunges around the track field for the whole class. But I have no firsthand knowledge of that because I took my sweet time walking to the health office.

I may not have been an alpha male, but I was an upper-classman. Comes with perks.

And then a year later, our PE teacher got fired. For other reasons.

The moral of this story is: Don't play bodies. And if you do, hit back.

Chapter 7

Laser Tag

In other states, summer vacation happens when the weather is at its best. In Arizona, the weather during this period of time is what we call: "Why do I live here?"

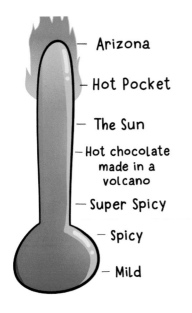

Arizona

Hot Pocket

The Sun

Hot chocolate made in a volcano

Super Spicy

Spicy

Mild

It's too hot to do anything outside but go to a pool or watch stuff melt.

Seriously, swimming is the one activity we can do without risking heatstroke (you just get to risk sunburns and skin cancer instead). The thing is, you can only mess around in a pool for so long before it gets boring.

Fortunately, we've got some fun indoor places that have air-conditioning. When I was little, my family and I went to Chuck E. Cheese's all the time. And nothing says good pizza and good times like a large robotic singing rodent.

When I got older, the best thing to do in the summers was to play laser tag. If you didn't know already, "laser" is actually an acronym for "light amplification by stimulated emission of radiation." So really, it should be "labseor" tag, but that doesn't sound as cool.

Nobel Prize winner Arthur Schawlow invented the laser in 1957 and, sure, lasers were used in the lunar landing and they have medical and military purposes, but I think we can all agree that their best application is laser pointers and laser tag.

Cats love LABSEOR pointers!

Lasers can supply you with hours of fun. Unless you're my coworker who was fired for shining a laser pointer at cars. Don't do that.

When I was about fifteen, I went with a group of my friends to a laser tag place for someone's birthday party. If you've never played laser tag, here's how it usually goes: When you get there, you have to wait for the game inside to finish up before you can play. Since sessions last thirty minutes, the place has arcade games to keep you busy and take more money from you.

So my friends and I were playing some arcade games, and this group of four guys came in wearing all black. I'm talking black long-sleeve shirts, black pants, and even black gloves. Three of them were wearing some sort of a black hat and the one who wasn't already had black hair.

They looked about eighteen or nineteen years old. So they were older than us, but still young enough to go all-out commando at a laser tag place.

My first thought was, *Ha! Look at these goths. They think they're all cool with their dark clothes. What dweebs.*

But then I remembered that the laser tag arena was dimly lit. These guys weren't goths; they were wearing camouflage.

So then I thought, *Wow, these guys came prepared.* But another part of me thought, *Wow, these guys are even **bigger** dweebs. They came prepared to a laser tag fight.*

I don't know what these guys' names were, but I'm going to call them all Hunter. Not because they were prepared to go out and "hunt" people, but because I think only someone with a name like Hunter would do this. It's just one of those names. If someone named Hunter is reading this . . . I'm not sorry.

Now, before a laser tag session starts, everyone has to sit in a room while some bored employee tells you, in a very scripted manner, the rules of the game. At one point, they make you repeat the rules back to them. They say, "I will not run, jump, or climb!"

And then you have to say, "I will not run, jump, or climb."

I remember while we were chanting the rules, these four guys were just staring off into space not repeating anything.

Maybe they thought they were too cool for rules.

Anyway, it was pretty clear they were planning on running, jumping, and/or climbing.

After we (excluding the Hunters) were all through repeating the rules, we went to a fairly large, multilevel arena. Some laser tag places are skimpy on the scenery, but this place had towers, pillars, and platforms to hide on. It even had mirrors to make things more confusing. All that was missing was a zipline and a teleporter. Then it would have been *really* awesome.

We all started playing the game. Everything was dark except—for some inexplicable reason—the vests we wore.

Those had colored lights on them to designate which team you were on. You could belong to one of three teams: the red team, the yellow team, or the blue or green team. I've forgotten the actual colors. That's not important.

So we were having fun fake-shooting people, when all of a sudden, I ran into this group of people wearing strobe lights on their shoulders. The lights were so bright they blocked out the colored lights on their vests, making them harder to hit. I couldn't see these guys' faces or really any-thing in their direction, but I knew immediately who these guys were. Do you wanna take a guess?

A.   The Hunters
B.   The Hunters
C.   A lightning bug having a seizure

That's right. It was the Hunters.

At first, I stood my ground and shot at the flashing field of light, but I got hit so many times, I broke one of the rules. I *ran* away.

Can you blame me? These kids came prepared. If we were using real lasers, I wouldn't have stood a chance. I found one of my friends and said, "Did you see the guys with the strobe lights?"

"Yeah," he said. "They gave me this scar." And he had a twelve-inch scar on his face.

I'm just kidding. That didn't happen. We were fighting with lasers. But can you imagine?

This meant war with the Hunters. After they'd pulled a move like that, I wasn't going to let them get away, untouched from my laser.

Later in the game, I went to one of the towers, got a good vantage point, and waited. This strategy is called "camping" and is universally frowned upon, but if the Hunters weren't going to play fair, neither would I. I saw a flashing light, followed by darkness, followed by another flashing light very quickly in the distance. And that's when the Hunters became the Huntered. I was going to straight-up *snipe* these dweebs. I started spamming my trigger.

I landed a hit. I knew I'd hit one of them because we got to make up names for ourselves before we started. And, well, no one took that seriously. We all came up with joke names like Buttfart or Big Wiener or ShootyMcShootface. But the name I chose was—

Let me explain. When you get shot, a screen on your gun says who shot you, so whenever I shot someone, their screen would say, "A girl shot your chest," or, "A girl shot your back." Sure, it's sexist, but at the time I thought it was the pinnacle of my comedy career.

I don't know if any of you guys have been in this situation, but let me tell you, it's very hard to keep a straight face when halfway across a laser tag arena an almost adult man screams with 100 percent seriousness,

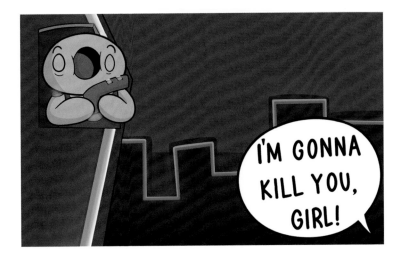

That was how I knew I'd hit someone. I was only a little intimidated by that threat. The rest of me was trying not to laugh. After I hit one of the Hunters, I ran away from my spot. (Another rule broken!)

So everything went on normally after that. We finished playing the game, and the lights turned on. While I was walking to the exit, I saw each of the Hunters holding a wad of black electrical tape. I'm not saying they put black tape over their sensors so you couldn't hit them,

but they totally put black electrical tape over their sensors so you couldn't hit them.

Luckily, though, their team didn't win, so *ha*!

Neither did my team, but that's not important. Can you imagine them in their car driving to the laser tag arena? Hunter is driving and he looks over and says, "Hunter, did you bring the strobe lights?"

"Yeah, Hunter. I brought them."

"Hunter, you got the tape, right?"

"Yeah, Hunter. It's right here."

"Hey, Hunter, where's your hat?"

"Hunter said he was going to bring me one."

"Oh, sorry, Hunter. I forgot."

"Here, Hunter, take my hat. My hair is already black."

"Thanks, Hunter."

I bet the ride home wasn't nearly as happy.

What I'm trying to tell you is, sometimes it doesn't matter who you are in life. You can plan. You can prepare. But A_Girl will always end up sniping you.

Chapter 8

Science Fair

I think we can all agree that schools make you learn a lot of useless stuff. People's usual go-to complaint about school is that we have to learn math. They'll say things like,

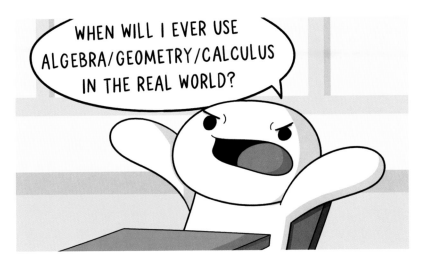

But why do so many people immediately point their finger at math? (I'm guessing because they're bad at algebra/geometry/calculus.) When will *I* ever have to use the things I learned in English class, like Shakespeare or iambic pentameter?

Once in fifth grade, my teacher called me to her desk, pointed to a spot in my homework, and said, "I asked you to write four methods the Hopi Indians used to dry farm their fields. You only wrote two."

My first thought was, Well, thank goodness I'm not a Hopi Indian dry farmer. I only know 50 percent of what they did.

And why does it even matter anymore? We have technology now. I bet the Hopi farmers today use sprinklers. So this isn't a problem I worry about.

I didn't actually say all that. And to tell you the truth, I've forgotten the two ways of dry farming I did put down, so that just shows how much I learned. I'm guessing water and some type of soil was involved.

But this chapter is about the school assignment that I hated the most:

THE SCIENCE FAIR

Once I was talking to my friend Jaiden about how much school science fairs suck. And she said, "Oh, at my school we didn't do the science fair."

That got me wondering whether other people had suffered through a science fair before. So I did my own science experiment: I ran a Twitter poll and asked if people had to do the science fair during school and whether they enjoyed doing it.

Of the 8,500 people who responded, 58 percent said that they didn't have to do a science fair. Which was way more than I'd expected. I've renamed this group the Lucky Ones.

Of those who did do the science fair, when asked whether they enjoyed it, 21 percent said they did—I'll call these people the Nerds—and 21 percent said they didn't. I know Twitter polls aren't the most accurate sources of data, but I think it's safe to say this issue is pretty evenly split.

I'm in the 21 percent of people who *didn't* enjoy the science fair. Don't get me wrong, I love science! Well, that may not be completely true. I really hated biology. It was just memorizing vocabulary words.

And chemistry, that was just a mess. Chemistry added even more vocabulary words and then tried to throw in math on top of everything else, and for some reason the periodic table was there too.

Fun fact about my AP chemistry class: At the start of the year, there was an even amount of boys and girls in the class, but then as the year went on, all the boys dropped the class until at the end of the year I was the only boy left. Which just goes to show you that chemistry is totally a ladies' club.

The only reason I passed chemistry was because I got some extra-credit points, which just meant the teacher didn't want to have to teach me again.

The only useful thing I did in that class was come up with the name for the comic I was going to create that summer: "theodd1sout."

I thought physics was okay. It was a good balance of math and vocabulary words. It really made me think about serious stuff, like:

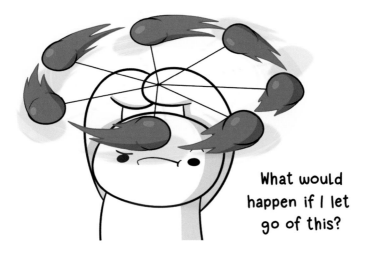

What would happen if I let go of this?

On second thought, maybe I don't like science; maybe I just liked watching *The Magic School Bus* and *Bill Nye the Science Guy*.

Anyway, let me briefly go over what the science fair is for you Lucky Ones who didn't have to do it. We started working on science fair projects around fourth grade, and did them every year up until tenth grade. Everyone in the class would spend a lot of time researching a topic that interested them, and then we all had to come up with a question about the topic that we could base an experiment on.

Here are the sorts of questions we chose:

Does the temperature of a battery affect how long it will last?

What color light produces the most heat?

How does the shape of a rocket's fins affect its travel?

All of these were projects I did. The science fair was supposed to teach us about the scientific method, but all it really taught me was to procrastinate and make up data. (Sorry, scientists.)

You might think, "Oh, but the science fair sounds like fun. I wish my school did them!"

Here were some of the flaws of the science fair:

First, we got the option to work with a partner. Working with a partner sounds like a good idea because you can split up the work and not do as much. Now, since I didn't have any friends, in fourth grade I partnered up with someone no one else wanted to be with. Unfortunately, he didn't do any of the work. He just blew off his part of the assignment.

That was enough to keep me from wanting to partner with anyone on anything ever again.

The second problem with the science fair was that we had to come up with a question to investigate all on our own. And you have to understand, we were just kids. We didn't exactly have the cognitive abilities that scientists have.

Just a couple of years before, we all still believed in Santa Claus (except for me—my family didn't do Santa Claus). Adults didn't even trust us with lockers in high school. And now teachers wanted us to wonder if the ratio of a cylinder would affect its buoyancy? Come on.

I think maybe it would have been better if we were assigned a question, at least in elementary school. I know the whole point of the project is to help us learn about the process of discovery, but we're all stupid when we're kids, all right?

Plus, we didn't have access to any research resources. The science fair is a lot like an episode of *MythBusters*, but what sets the MythBusters apart from your average fourth grader is that they have access to high-end explosives and TV production money, while we have to ask our parents to drive us to Walmart for art supplies.

Hey mom...

One time I wanted to do an experiment on a certain type of soil, so I did research and came up with a question, but then when my mom and I went to Home Depot, they didn't have the correct soil, so I had to start over and make up a whole new question. I bet the MythBusters never have to do that. Their moms would take them to a different Home Depot.

Which shows you that if you choose a crappy question for your project, you will automatically have a bad experience. For my very first science fair, after spending a day research- ing possible questions, my partner and I came up with this:

Now, I already know the answer to this question, and in fourth grade, I'm sure I knew the answer too. It's noon. (*Editor's note: Actually, it's around three p.m.*) I don't need to run an experiment on that. In fact, I can go to Google, type in "weather," and—boom—there are my results right there. No need for an experiment.

But the science fair isn't about just finding the answer to your question, like regular science. No, no, no, no. After you research the topic, you have to write a hypothesis. A hypothesis is basically you guessing what you think the results of the experiment will be, but instead of writing, "I think this will happen," you have to write it like you *know* what the answer is. So basically the science fair is teaching you to lie.

The hottest time of the day is 8PM!

The formula for a perfect hypothesis is "If [blank] then [blank] because [blank]."

Let's use this formula for the battery experiment I did in sixth grade.

I asked, "Does the temperature of a battery affect how long it will last?" After doing research about how batteries work, and feeling confident about what the results should be, we'd write a hypothesis for this experiment like this: "**If** two double A batteries are used at differing temperatures **then** the battery in the hot temperature will not last as long **because** the battery's fluid will evaporate, which damages the internal structure of the battery."

Oh, and spoiler alert, no, no, it doesn't. I put two batteries outside on a hot day and two in the freezer, let them sit, and when I plugged them into my Game Boy Advance they lasted the exact same amount of time.

The upside of this experiment was that I got to play my Game Boy Advance and call it homework.

For the science fair report, you also have to write up the materials used, the steps to do your experiment (the "procedures"), and an introduction. The introduction is basically you writing about what you're going to do.

Then you do the experiment, a.k.a. the *fun* part. Make sure you write down your results (the not fun part), because you have to graph them. How do you make a graph to show that your batteries at different temperatures lasted the same amount of time?

You think you're done, right? But you're not. Now you have to write up your results as if your graph didn't already perfectly depict the results *and* write a conclusion. The conclusion is

the most insulting part of the science fair. You basically answer this list of questions:

Was your hypothesis correct?

No, my hypothesis was not correct.

What mistakes might you have made in your experiment?

Possible mistake:

*I don't know! Maybe I took the batteries out of the cold
and hot places too soon and I put them in a room-tempera-
ture Game Boy so that in a couple minutes they both were at
room temperature again.*

How can others use the information you found?

*What do you mean? All the batteries lasted the same
amount of time! I don't think anyone is going to put their
batteries in their freezer to have literally no effect.*

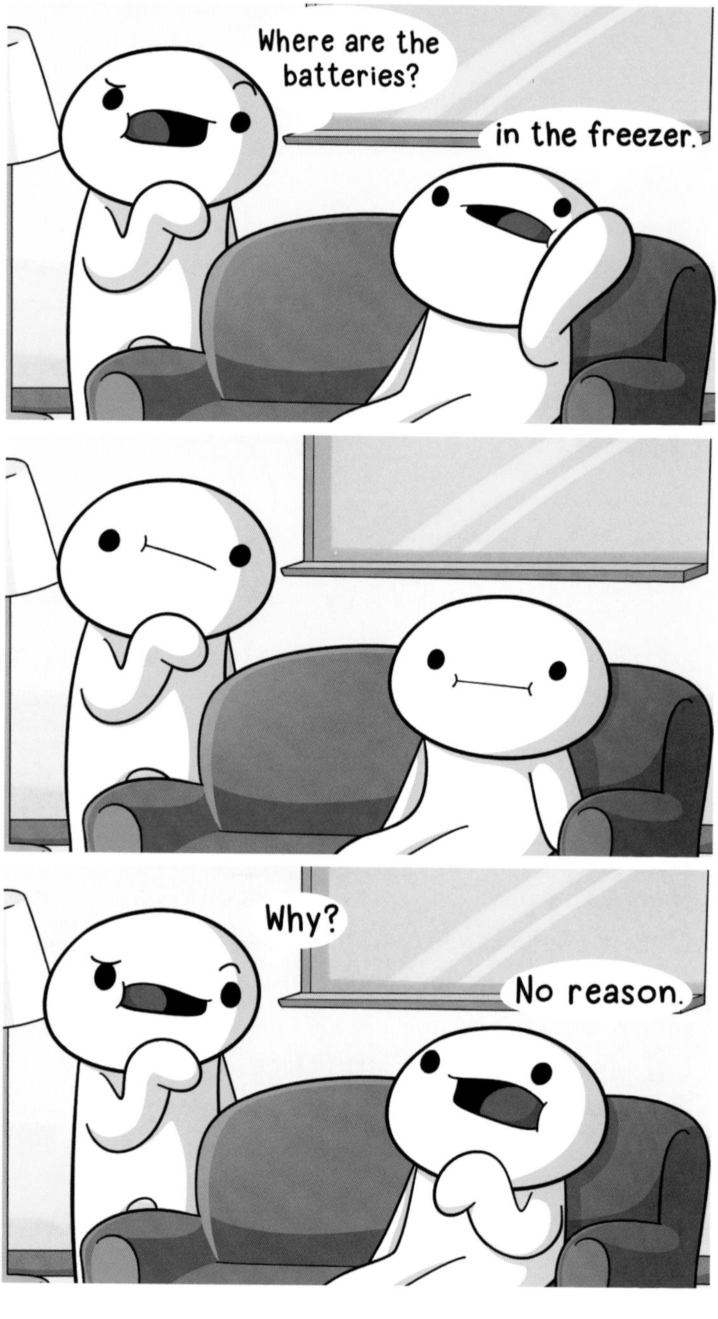
Where are the batteries?
in the freezer.
Why?
No reason.

Another year, I wanted to do a project to see if plants could grow from reflected light. I never ended up doing this one because of one simple problem: This is a project that can't be procrastinated. Plants take a while to grow. I'm going to guess ("hypothesize") and say, yeah, they probably can grow from reflected light. I don't think plants check to see if light has bounced off a mirror first before photosynthesizing it. I mean, I've seen potatoes sprout to life in the darkness of a pantry cupboard.

Anyway, after you're done writing down your data, you take everything you wrote, print it out, and then slap it onto a poster board. And everyone, and I mean *everyone*, used construction paper as a border around the text to give the poster board a good aesthetic.

The second most fun part of the science fair was choosing what Word Art font to use for your title.

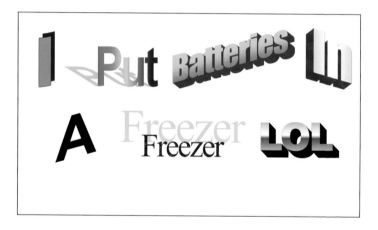

The teachers told us to have a creative title to catch people's attention—like that was part of the assignment. Basically, they were grading us on our ability to come up with puns. If you were doing a project about measuring plant growth, "Ready, Set, Grow" was a very popular choice.

And then everyone took their poster board to the front of the class and gave a presentation. Those were the three most boring days of science class ever. Except for the day you yourself presented. That was the most stressful day.

In all my years of listening to other kids talk about their science fair projects, I only remember one of them. There was this kid who did his project on water cleanliness, so he had a water meter that read the amount of total dissolved solids, or TDS, in the water. He must have had dyslexia, because during his presentation he talked about the STDs in the water. You really don't want to know how many STDs there were in the school drinking fountain.

Anyway, after presentations were finished, everyone in the school put their poster boards in the cafeteria and walked around to judge what people in other classes had done and how they'd decorated their poster boards.

And you could always tell whose mom had helped.

Overall, I did not have a good time. To those 21 percent of people who did enjoy the science fair, I'm glad you liked it, but me and the other 21 percent of people think you're huge nerds.

After I ran that Twitter poll, I had some people message me saying, "Yeah, I got third place and all I had was a cup of dirt, ha-ha!"

I think the key to a good science fair is to come up with a good question and also to do it on a topic you actually enjoy. One of my science fair projects was on rockets and I had a blast. (That would have been a good poster board title.) I actually chose that topic after I procrastinated on the "Can plants grow from reflected light?" idea. I had to come up with something that could be done fast, and "How does the shape of a rocket's fins affect its travel?" was easy because my older sister had already done this exact project.

And also my older brother did that project too.

You'd think I'd know a lot about rockets now, since my whole family has been around them, but all I really remember is that you shouldn't mess with a rocket's fins. They were probably designed by, I don't know, rocket scientists.

And no, I didn't just reuse my siblings' poster boards and data. My dad made me actually launch rockets.

Basically, working on the science fair is a lot like life. Choose your partner carefully, ask the right questions, and after you procrastinate, just launch model rockets.

Chapter 9

Son, It's Time We Talk About the Crickets and the Worms

After the traumatic kindergarten moth incident, I decided I wasn't a fan of insects anymore. But sometimes you can't avoid them.

Like, one time, I volunteered to watch a friend's pet frogs while he was away on vacation. Along with a frog habitat, he gave me a box of feeder crickets. Sadly, after the first day, I didn't put the lid securely onto the box and all the crickets escaped. Yeah.

Look, I never claimed to be super responsible.

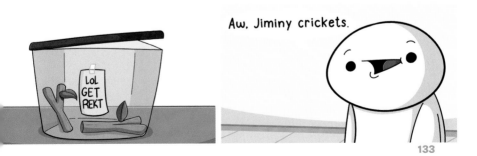

This was bad for two reasons:

1. Now we had nothing to feed the frogs; and
2. There were a bunch of rogue crickets in my bedroom.

Luckily, crickets make a loud noise at all times for no reason, so you'll always know that, yes, you do indeed have crickets in your bedroom. It was like they were taunting me.

We tried to put the crickets back in their prison, but it turns out, they didn't want to be eaten.

So we ended up using the vacuum.

But even with that method, we didn't catch all of them. After the loud vacuum turned off, the crickets seemed to think it was their turn to be as loud as possible. Those were tough nights.

Hopefully they all starved to death.

Don't feel sorry for those crickets, though. Their one and only purpose in life was to be food for amphibians, and they got to survive. Since all of the food had escaped, my family caught wild crickets outside to keep the frogs from starving.

But I don't want to talk about insects anymore. Instead, I'm going to tell you another rescue and release story. About worms. Which is only a small step up from insects. They're pretty much pink caterpillars that don't have a cool final evolution.

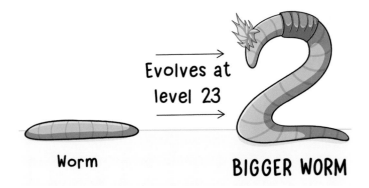

Evolves at level 23

Worm

BIGGER WORM

Has anyone ever told you that if a worm gets cut in half, it turns into two worms? Well, it turns out that's a myth. The only worms that have that superpower are planarian flatworms, which don't even look like worms.

PLANARIAN FLATWORM

I live in the desert of Arizona. Even the early birds here don't get the worms because worms aren't native to the desert. This is because the soil here is basically dry dirt and clay.

Here's a fun factoid: A little way down in the ground, we have a layer of cement-like soil called caliche. Caliche is so dense, the Native Americans who lived in Arizona used it to build their houses. The Casa Grande Ruins in Coolidge are still standing after seven hundred years.

The point being: Any soil that can be used to construct a centuries-old two-story house isn't going to be good for growing things. You can dig a hole and plant a tree, but that tree's roots aren't going to make it through the caliche. They will run across your lawn and tap on your window asking for a drink before they'll dig through the caliche.

So if you want to grow things like a garden or trees in Arizona, you have to improve the soil. The best way to do this is to buy new soil and throw it on the ground.

But there are other methods too. You can also compost, mulch, fertilize, and aerate, before you give up and buy new soil.

My parents have always had delusions about growing a garden. They've done all of the above in an attempt to grow tomatoes. It never really worked, though.

One day my mom and I were out walking in a neighboring subdivision and it happened to be raining. In other states when it rains, people stay inside and wait it out, hoping for better weather. In Arizona, people happily rush outside and start singing, or if they're in their car, they try to remember how to work their windshield wipers.

While we were walking outside in the rain, we happened to notice that there were worms on the sidewalk in front of one particular house. These people had obviously imported worms from a store to improve their landscaping.

According to a nature website I read once, worms are often called "nature's plow." They burrow through the ground and aerate the soil, which lets in water and oxygen. If they hit hard earth, they eat it. How many of you can say that about your problems? Worms eat organic matter and poop out their weight every day. And worm poop makes good soil. Think about that the next time you eat something that grew from the ground.

But worms aren't intelligent creatures. Throw a little water on them and they'll crawl out of the safety of their dirt homes and try their luck in the middle of a road. That's just never going to end well. Worms can't drive.

And so as we stood in front of this house, some of "nature's plows" were hurrying to their death by traveling away from the dirt and into the road.

My mom thought it would be a good idea to try to ~~steal~~ save some of the worms and use them for our garden,

which at the time was growing mostly tumbleweeds.

Hey, it's not stealing somebody's worms if they're on a death march (crawl) to the middle of the street. We were *rescuing* them.

At any rate, when we came home from the walk, my mom told me to take a bowl, drive back over to that subdivision, and get some of the worms for our garden.

Perhaps the saddest thing about this story is that this isn't even the strangest request I've gotten from my parents. I didn't want to do it, but I'm a good son, so I got an old bowl and drove over.

At first, things went well. I parked the car, I walked over to where the worms were fleeing—they're not that fast so it's not that hard to catch them—and, using a stick, I scooped up a bunch of worms and put them into the bowl. Worm rescue accomplished. And if the neighbors looked out, they would probably think,

"Hey, it's that weird kid who used to come out every night to catch crickets. Is he stealing our worms now too?"

I put the bowl on the seat beside me and started to drive home.

The thing about worms is that when you touch them with a stick, they roll up into a circle and play dead. I guess they think this makes them less appetizing to predators. But actually, any animal who would eat a worm in the first place is probably not going to be that picky about eating one that's been dead for a few seconds.

So at first all of the worms were calmly playing dead in the bowl, but as I drove down the street, they seemed to come to the realization that they didn't need to play dead anymore.

And all of them began trying to escape from the bowl.

For creatures who are stupid enough to go charging into a street to take on cars, they're pretty good at escaping from bowls.

I should have realized that if worms are good at climbing up out of the ground, of course they would be good at climbing out of a bowl.

While I was driving, I looked over and noticed that several of them were halfway out.

I did what anybody in that situation would do: I screamed. Then I drove the car with one hand while simultaneously trying to shake the worms back into the bowl. This is not a good driving technique, especially if it happens to be raining and you still don't know how to work the windshield wipers.

Some of you are probably thinking, "James, your life's not worth a bunch of worms." But the thing is, I couldn't focus on driving while I knew that every passing second another worm was escaping and probably going to rot underneath the seats.

Besides, I was going out with friends later and I didn't want to have to say, "Hey, in case you feel anything wet and slimy slithering around your seat, it's just a bunch of worms."

So, yes, I drove home one-handed while shaking the bowl to get a bunch of worms to play dead again.

When I finally got to my house, I went to the backyard and threw them in the garden, and I never saw them again. I don't even know if they were smart enough to stick around and burrow into the ground or if they headed straight toward the street and their impending deaths again. Maybe the early birds showed up and got them.

The garden didn't really get any better after that so it's hard to tell.

Some people ask me why I always end my YouTube videos with the phrase, "Wear your seatbelt."

Experiences like this are probably why.

Chapter 10

Georgie vs. the Chihuahua

One of the most frustrating things about owning a dog is that you can't ask them questions.

Why do you hate laundry baskets so much?

The most important question I wish I could ask my dog, Georgie, is: Why do you hate Chihuahuas?

Georgie is fine with other dogs. Maybe it's because she's on the small-dog end of the canine spectrum and doesn't want to tick off bigger dogs.

The only dog breed that Georgie hates is Chihuahuas. I don't know what Chihuahuas ever did to her, but she hates them with an intense and persistent passion.

Georgie is a Westie, and those were bred to kill rodents, so I guess it is entirely possible that Georgie is so stupid she can't tell the difference between a Chihuahua and a rat.

SAME THING

This wouldn't be much of a problem, except that a neighbor who lives a few streets down from us has a Chihuahua. I'm pretty sure my dog thinks our neighbor is out walking her pet rodent every day.

Whatever the case, Georgie has decided that the Chihuahua is her archnemesis.

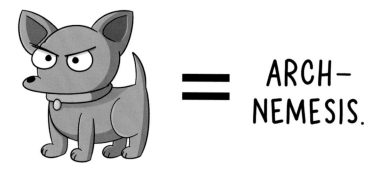

= ARCH-NEMESIS.

The first time I found out about this relationship, my older brother had just come home from work and was in the driveway getting things out of his car. Georgie stood by the front window barking frantically. I thought she was just excited that Luke had come home and wanted to see him. I opened the door, expecting Georgie to trot over to Luke. Instead, she completely ignored him and dashed across the yard to our neighbor, who we'll now refer to as the Chihuahua Lady, out walking Archnemesis.

I was surprised, but not worried. Georgie has always gotten along with every other dog she's met. In fact, our family
became friends with another neighborhood family because
every time she sees their dog, Coco, in the park, she barks
until we take her there. This social visit usually involves Georgie sniffing Coco's butt and peeing wherever she thinks
Coco has peed. This is what best friends do. So Georgie gets
along with others.

Anyway, I was just about to call out to the Chihuahua Lady and tell her not to worry because Georgie is a friendly dog, when I saw my dog transform into Satan.

The lady tried to protect her Chihuahua by yanking its leash so that the dog was lifted off the ground. Little Arch-nemesis was barking and yapping and trying to bite Georgie, because apparently, he'd never noticed that every other dog is bigger than him. The Chihuahua Lady kept turning her body away from Georgie, and Georgie kept chasing after her dog, until the Chihuahua was basically airborne and swinging around like he was hooked on to a ceiling fan.

I don't know why she didn't just pick her dog up.

Don't worry, the Chihuahua was fine. I think.

I finally reached my dog, picked her up, and apologized. "I've never seen her act this way," I said. "I don't know what got into her."

The Chihuahua Lady was understandably upset. "Your dog has already done this once before," she told me. "Your little sister had your dog at the park and she tried to attack my dog there."

I wouldn't have believed that story if I hadn't just seen my dog act like she was possessed by demons. I apologized some more, hauled Georgie inside, and gave her a stern talking-to.

    I'd like to say that the story ends here, and my dog was well-behaved after that, but no. That's not what happened. There's still a lot left in this chapter.

    Georgie, for whatever canine reason, decided it was her job to eradicate all Chihuahuas from the neighborhood. Every time my sister and I took her on a walk and we passed the Chihuahua Lady's house, Georgie went ballistic. She barked and pulled on the leash until she was choking herself—

again, I never claimed she was a smart dog—and she insisted on peeing on the sidewalk in front of her archnemesis's house, repeatedly. Because Georgie wanted the Chihuahua to know she'd been by.

A couple of times when we opened the door to let someone in, Georgie ran outside and sped off toward the Chihuahua Lady's house. We always caught her by the gate trying to tunnel her way into their backyard. Anytime she tried to do that, we put her in her kennel as punishment. She knew that this was bad behavior, but she never seemed to care.

And then one day when my parents were out of town and I was in charge, things got worse. This is probably an indication that I should not be in charge. At least not in charge of my little sister, Arianna, and my sometimes-demon-possessed dog.

My sister had taken Georgie to the park with her friend and for some reason—the reason being that she doesn't listen to instructions—Arianna let Georgie off the leash so the dog could sniff around while Arianna and her friend played. According to my sister, she was *about* to put Georgie's leash back on, when suddenly Georgie's ears perked up and she took off running.

Mind you, this is a dog who frequently cannot find a piece of hot dog that has been thrown to her on the floor.

However, she could apparently pick up the scent of the Chihuahua from a quarter-mile away.

He's here.

My sister chased after her, but even the smallest dog can outrun the fastest person. And Arianna isn't the fastest person. It makes no sense. People have much longer legs and are stronger too, but nearly every other animal in the world is faster than us.

My sister didn't have a chance of catching our dog. Georgie reached the Chihuahua, a fight ensued, and the Chihuahua did not do well. By the time my sister pulled Georgie off the other dog, he was bleeding. Everyone was very upset about this—except for Georgie.

The Chihuahua Lady was furious, and my sister was in tears.

Arianna took Georgie home, put Georgie in her kennel, and gave her another one of those stern lectures that are completely wasted on our dog.

A few minutes later, the Chihuahua Lady rang our door-bell. When Arianna answered, the Chihuahua Lady asked to speak to her parents.

Arianna said, "My parents are out of town."

"Who is in charge while they're gone?" the Chihuahua Lady asked.

"My older brother," Arianna said.

(That's me.)

I had nothing to do with this whole ordeal. I was at improv practice at the time, but suddenly I was responsible for my possessed dog and my sister, who'd let a demon loose on the world.

The Chihuahua Lady said she'd be back and threatened to call the police because we couldn't control our dog.

I mean, sure, this was the third time Georgie had attacked Archnemesis and the Chihuahua Lady had every right to be mad at Georgie. But you don't need to arrest a dog.

My sister called me while I was at improv practice and told me what had happened. And while my sister talked, all I could think was: The police are going to come, take away my dog, and send her to dog jail. Maybe they'll even put her down. And I'm the one in charge of everything while my parents are out of town. I'm the one who's going to have to bail Georgie out of dog jail. She's going to have a record. She'll never be able to hold down a job now. Or worse, I'm going to have to explain to my parents that we no longer have a dog.

I remembered hearing somewhere that the police can't come into your house unless they have a warrant.

I don't know whether this applies in the case of dog attacks, because I don't have a lot of experience with law enforcement. (Take my word for it.)

I figured, if we just didn't let the police inside, then they couldn't take our dog. This strategy was our best option, at least until our parents came home and dealt with the problem. Then it would be *their* problem.

I told my sister, "If the police come to the house, don't let them in."

"Okay," she said.

But she obviously had a problem listening to instructions or she wouldn't have let the dog off the leash in the first place, so I felt the need to repeat myself with louder, more specific instructions. "If someone knocks on the door, look out the peephole. If anyone on the doorstep looks like the police or a SWAT team or is wearing a uniform of any kind, do not open the door!"

Right after I said all this, I realized there are certain things you shouldn't say in a crowded area.

1. *The doctor says my highly contagious diarrhea will last for months.*

2. *My pet crocodile got loose again.*

And lastly,

3. *If the police show up at the house, don't let them in.*

No one on my improv team asked what was going on. They clearly thought I lived a pretty rad life and were too afraid to ask.

Fortunately, the police never showed up.

In case you're reading this book right now, thank you, Chihuahua Lady, for not sending Georgie to dog jail. I'm sorry that she keeps trying to kill your dog.

A couple of years later, we got our second dog, Poppy, from a shelter. She's frequently demonic around us, especially if you try to pick her up, but the upside is that she hasn't tried to kill any other dogs (yet). Unlike Georgie, whose ancestors were bred to kill vermin, Poppy was bred for only one thing: looking cute. It is the only skill she has.

On the downside, Poppy will never protect us in an attack. She would lick invaders instead of biting them, and our cats could beat her up if they wanted. But at least we don't have to worry about the police taking her to dog jail. That's where we got her from. She's already done her time.

So what I'm saying is, get a dog that was bred to be a low achiever. They'll get you into less trouble.

Chapter 11

My Haunting Haunted House Hour

Why do we like scary things? Fear isn't a good emotion. If we were all given a choice between being afraid and not being afraid, I feel like "not being afraid" should be everyone's choice. But for some reason people still pay money to watch scary movies and go to haunted houses.

How did people even come up with the idea for the first haunted house?

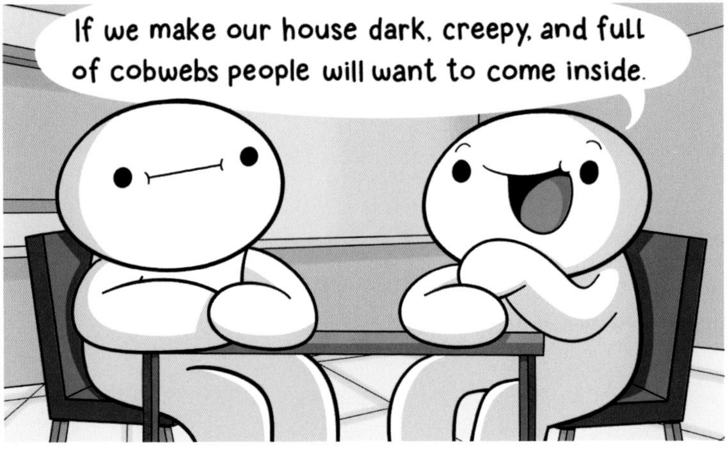
If we make our house dark, creepy, and full of cobwebs people will want to come inside.

I think haunted houses are fine. I don't want to brag or anything, but since the age of sixteen, I've never been in a haunted house that scared me. Granted, all the haunted houses I've been in were free, and didn't make me sign a waiver.

I will admit that I was terrified of haunted houses as a little kid. Once when I was trick-or-treating, I came across a house where they'd turned their garage into a haunted house—or in this case, a haunted garage.

I walked in, saw someone lying on the floor like they were dead, and I turned around and ran all the way home. Halloween was over.

But after that, whenever I saw a haunted house, I kept telling myself that none of the things I was seeing were real. And when I grew up, that idea stuck with me.

When you realize the severed hand is made of plastic, all the tension you previously felt disappears. Or maybe I don't get scared 'cause I just don't feel emotions anymore, who knows. Anyway, I still get startled at the jump scares, but since they don't stab you or anything, it's always awkward afterward.

I'm just going to go this way now.

Not stuff I should be afraid of:	Real stuff I should be afraid of:
- vampires. - ghosts. - zombies. - people who stand around waving their arms while their guts are hanging out.	death. taxes.

That said, there is one haunted house experience that happened during my senior year of high school that I'll never forget. It was probably one of the most traumatizing things I've ever seen, and also, it's hard to forget it because I made a video about it.

During my senior year, I was part of the drama club. Each October, the school put on a fair, probably to raise money or something. It seems that schools are always in need of extra cash.

The football team got to do the dunk tank, the band kids did face painting, and the theater kids put on a haunted house, which is way more interesting than face painting or dunk tanking, if you ask me. Well, maybe not the dunk tank. That was fun.

The drama club got to set up the haunted house inside the school. We separated into groups and each was part of a scary attraction. My group dressed up as vampires and sat at a dinner table. We decorated it with fake organs and goblets filled with blood (red Kool-Aid) and we had a freshman girl dramatically sprawled across the table. She had a mush of fake organs coming out of her stomach.

We sat around and pretended we were eating her, because vampires eat . . . okay, now that I think about it, our attraction didn't make any sense. Why would a group of vampires be eating someone? They don't do that. Plus, why would they go to a high school? That's a dumb idea. Hope no one turns that into a book.

Anyway, we put a yellow sheet over the ceiling light for a good spooky atmosphere. We had a smoke machine, some ambient Halloween music playing—we were pretty legit. Whenever a group of people walked by, we would just silently stare at them, and then the freshman on the table would scream at the top of her lungs. Since we had so much space in between each of the scary attractions, when people walked past, we would all get up and chase them. It was awesome. Hours of screaming and chasing people.

This wouldn't be on most people's bucket list, but don't knock it until you try it.

Bucket list

1) See the pyramids
2) Climb Mt. Everest
3) Lay on a table with pool
   noodles and scream for hours

Theater kids are very loud, extroverted people, so we were the type of kids who thrived on screaming and chasing. Especially this one kid in my vampire group. We'll name him, uh, Balake.

Balake was pretty crazy. He was loud; it seemed like he was *always* yelling. I didn't have any classes with him, but he was obviously a high-self-esteem, class-clown kinda kid.

After we'd done the haunted house for about two hours, we were all getting tired of it. I want you to think about what it's like to be inside a haunted house. With all the strobe lights, the smoke, and the freshman who was constantly screaming bloody murder—you did a good job, freshman—the sensory overload starts to wear on you. These days just going into a haunted house for five minutes makes me feel uncomfortable, sweaty, and dizzy.

We were supposed to get a break sometime in the middle of the night, but since the haunted house was so popular, we didn't get any breaks. None. So we were all a little loopy after doing this stuff for so long.

This group of people walked in, and we did our normal thing. We got up and chased them. But Balake got pretty physical with this one little boy. Like he kinda shook him up a bit. And I didn't see exactly what happened, but this little boy was holding a fish in a plastic baggy.

It was one of those little tiny fish that are supposed to be used as food for bigger fish. A lot of fairs give them away as prizes. Ninety-nine percent of the time the fish die within two weeks because you don't have the right aquarium equipment. So you just put them in water and watch them slowly die. You know—those fish.

I didn't think people were allowed to bring their new pet fish into the haunted house, but I guess the boy smuggled it in or something.

Anyway, I didn't see the kid drop the fish. Maybe Balake slapped it out of his hands. But I heard a scream and I saw a fish flopping around in a puddle on the floor.

Fish look like they're in so much pain when they're out of water. I don't flail around uncontrollably when I go swimming.

So I was silently panicking because the fish looked like he was going to die in three seconds if we didn't do something. I tried to think of places that we could put the fish, like, uh, the toilet.

But without saying anything, Balake bent down, cupped the tiny fish in his hands, then ran back to the table. He put the fish in an empty goblet and poured red Kool-Aid into the cup.

Naw, I'm just kidding. He got a water bottle from under the table that the teacher had given us. The fish was fine, ladies and gentlemen. Thanks to Balake's quick thinking, he saved this little kid's fish.

The kid was still a couple feet down the hall. Balake took the goblet in his hands, walked it over to the kid, reached out his hand to give the kid his fish back . . . BUT THEN INSTEAD OF HANDING OVER THE FISH, HE JUST CHUGGED THE DRINK!

HE. DRANK. THE. FISH!!

The kid let out the most bloodcurdling scream. It sounded like he'd just watched his pet get swallowed by a stranger. Honestly, it was the loudest scream I heard that night. I bet the people in the next group behind this one were, like, "Oh, man, I bet whatever's next must be really scary!"

The kid tried to attack Balake, and I'm sure if he had the correct tools, he would have murdered him. Balake eventually spat out the fish. He didn't swallow it. *Thankfully* it was just swimming in his mouth.

But I mean, that's what you've got to do when you're working in a haunted house. You have to scare people any way you can. I'm certain that kid will be scarred for life. I was just a bystander and I still wake up in a cold sweat thinking about it.

Turned out, this kid was actually Balake's little brother. So at least Balake didn't do this to a complete stranger. Man, you've got to appreciate the lengths older brothers go to in order to torment their little brothers.

Balake's little brother, if you're reading this, first of all, thanks for buying the book. Second, I was there, dude. I know the pain you went through. I have an older brother too. I know what it's like to be Luigi.

At least my older brother never swallowed any of my pets. He just stole my food, so there's that.

He also never let me win in Super Smash Bros. Anytime I was about to win, he would turn off the Nintendo.

But I mean, I'm fiiine. Look how great I turned out.

I guess this is where I should say something philosophical about overcoming your fears. You should always face your fears. Don't run away from your own personal haunted garages. That does nothing but ruin Halloween and keep you from getting more candy. And remember, your family will always be there for you. Although, that could be what you're afraid of.

Chapter 12

Job Interviews:
A Traumatic Rite of Passage

Job interviews are a painful rite of passage. Do you have too much self-esteem? A job interview can help you with that.

When I was a teen, all the cool kids had jobs. They made money so they could afford to go out and do stuff. I didn't really want to go out and do stuff, but my parents still thought I should get a job. As soon as I turned sixteen, my dad started asking me,

And I would answer, "Do I look like my soul has been crushed? No? Then no, I didn't get a job." Okay, I never said that. But he kept asking.

Granted, it's important to get a job so you can save money for college. I thought that was the main reason people my age were employed, but when I finally did get a job, only one other person I worked with was planning on going to college.

I don't know what my coworkers did with their money, but I suspect there may have been drugs involved. Some things you just don't ask.

Here's my advice to teens: Even though you won't be able to afford college after working at a minimum wage job, get one anyway, because every penny helps. College is *important* . . . except in my case. I dropped out of college.

Anyway, during my search for employment, I applied to places online, but then my dad told me that I needed to apply in person because that way was better. Managers needed to see my sparkling, responsible face. But 99 percent of the time when I walked into some minimum wage establishment and asked some teenage employee for an application, that person would look at me like I was an idiot and say, "You know, you can do that online, right?"

One of the first places I applied to was Cold Stone Creamery, because I thought: I like ice cream. Ice cream will be a good fit for me. I could totally live at an ice cream place.

A manager called me and said, "Here at Cold Stone, we like to do things a little differently."

Their idea of "a little differently" was that they invited twelve kids in at the same time for a group interview. I went in for the interview wearing my job interview polo shirt, nervous but with high expectations. We sat at a table and took turns saying an interesting thing about ourselves, sort of like that game teachers make you play when they're trying to be fun and have everyone get to know each other in class. Let me say, I hate trying to think of an interesting thing about myself. What am I supposed to say that's more interesting than these other eleven people? Will I be better at scooping ice cream if I'm more interesting?

The guy who was leading the interview told us that Cold Stone liked outgoing, smiling people. I thought my interesting fact could be that I did improv, but then I thought, No, that would be bragging. I bet they like outgoing, smiling, *humble* people.

So instead my interesting fact was

Which apparently isn't interesting enough.

Then the Cold Stone guy broke us into two groups and had us sing some *quality* Cold Stone songs. Basically, what they did was take popular songs and insert ice cream terminology into them. This should have been my first clue that job interviews would be humiliating. We weren't assigned a leader, but I totally led my group, showing initiative. Really, they should have hired me on the spot.

The song we chose to sing was a parody of Queen's "We Will Rock You." Although I'm hesitant to call it a parody, because "parody" would imply that it's going to be funny.

The words were:

The song would have been better if the lyrics were: "We will, we will, rocky road you." Just saying, Cold Stone.

I was hoping that at some point in the interview the manager would give us all ice cream. But no. We sang for nothing. And they never called to offer me a job.

Next, I applied to be a server at a nursing home. I went in wearing my "Hire me" polo shirt again, and the manager told me that he would need more information about me, including my blood type and a drug test. Here's the second thing I learned from job interviews: If a place wants your blood type, maybe they require more than you're willing to give. I'm still not sure why they wanted that piece of information.

But I knew what blood type I was because I've donated blood. Remember how I said I didn't want to brag before? This time I totally bragged. "Yeah, I save lives in my spare time. I'm a great person."

I didn't get that job either.

Why is it so difficult to get hired in fast food or retail? If you don't have any friends that are working someplace that's hiring, and if you don't have any past job experience, then it's way too hard. Or maybe I just completely failed every single interview. I dunno.

I applied to who knows how many places. There was only a 20 percent chance that they would call to set up an interview. And then after the interview, there was a 0 percent chance that they would hire me.

Can we talk about those insulting personality quizzes they make you take? How are places supposed to know whether you're a good worker from a quiz? When I first started applying to places, I answered those questions truthfully. But then when I got desperate, I just answered "strongly agree" or "strongly disagree" every time. My opinions were never "somewhat." I never had a neutral opinion.

I really hate this!! I really like this!!

One time I applied to a grocery store. This woman took me into the break room, told me to wait there, and then left. She was gone for twenty minutes. Yes, I timed it, because the only thing I had to look at while I waited was a clock. I didn't want to start playing on my phone just in case she walked back in and saw how irresponsible I was being. So I just sat there, doing nothing, for twenty minutes. I honestly thought she'd forgotten about me.

How long are you supposed to sit in a break room before you just awkwardly get up and leave? They don't teach you that kind of stuff in school.

What to do if you're left in a break room during a job interview.

While I sat in the break room, other employees were just walking in and out. None of them acknowledged my existence. Which makes me wonder, does that mean I could just walk into any other break room and sit down and no one would stop me or ask why I was there?

Finally, the lady came back with another girl. This girl was being trained to be a manager so the lady was using me to teach her how to interview people. They sat across from me at the table and the lady said stuff like, "So you can't ask him if he's eighteen. You have to ask him if he's *over* eighteen."

Then the girl looked at me and said, "Are you over eighteen?"

The lady leaned over toward the girl, pointing at a form. "Okay, so you're going to check the 'do not hire' box right there."

Then I applied to a Chipotle and I freaking got an interview, right? They didn't hire me, obviously. But then I applied to a different Chipotle and I got an interview there too. But I guess the first Chipotle snitched on me because when I got to the second Chipotle, the manager lady there asked me, "Did you already apply here?"

I said, "I interviewed at a different Chipotle."

She sat me down and started telling me about how Chipotle was looking for a *certain type* of person to work for them.

All I heard was,

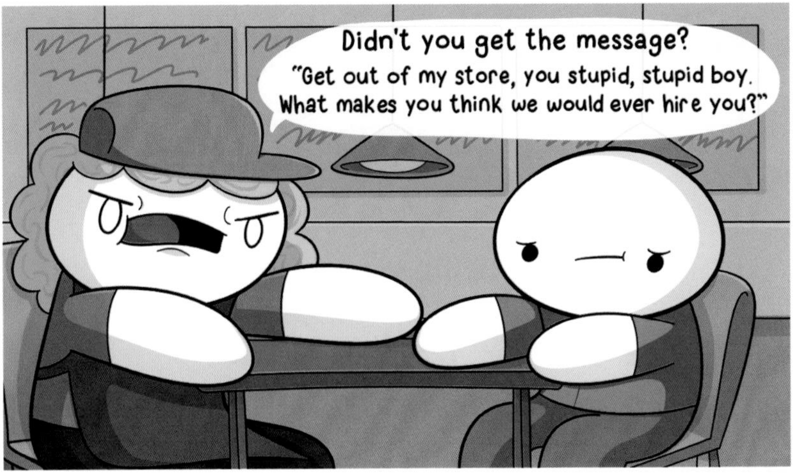
Didn't you get the message?
"Get out of my store, you stupid, stupid boy. What makes you think we would ever hire you?"

Pfft . . . "certain type."

What—were they looking for people who could successfully put all the sour cream on one half of the burrito? Was that what she meant by "certain type"? Because there seem to be an excess number of employees at every Chipotle who are that "certain type."

Apparently, I was the "certain type" of person who worked at "Sooubway," because that's where I finally got hired. I'm not sure if that's an insult or not.

And okay, I don't want to *brag*, but I was one of the best employees that Sooubway ever had. I was always on time or five minutes late, no in between. I never called in at the last minute saying I needed someone to cover my shift. In fact, I think I covered the most shifts. And whenever I closed with another person, the manager would usually complain about the work the other person did, because my work was always perfect.

So all those places that didn't hire me, you missed out!

The best employee ever that you missed out on.

(That's me)

One day, after working at Sooubway for a while, I decided that I didn't want to be a sandwich artist anymore and I didn't want to keep being paid minimum wage.

I actually like math. I'm pretty freaking smart. (I have a job now, so I can brag.) I applied to be a math tutor at my community college. That would have been the perfect job. I was a math education major, I wanted to be a math teacher, and this job would give me good practice for the actual job.

In this interview, the other math tutors gave me a practice problem and then had me "teach" it back to them. This sort of interview makes sense. I think all jobs should have a "practice round" instead of an interview.

I was standing in front of a whiteboard. For some stupid reason, I was only allowed to teach up to the level of math that I had completed.

I did AP calculus in high school but for another stupid reason the credits didn't transfer. Maybe it was because I didn't take the AP test, who knows. I had to do calculus all over again in community college.

So when I was applying for this job, I could only tutor algebra and trigonometry. I got my practice problem, and it was obviously a calculus problem. It was one of these: This is Person A's distance over time and this is Person B's distance over time. Who was going faster at this time? And okay, this is an easy problem. Take my word for it. But since the people I was quote-unquote *tutoring* didn't know calculus, I couldn't use calculus to teach them.

I asked, "Do you guys know what a derivative is?"

They looked at each other and said,

I did my dang darned best trying to teach them what calculus was, but then when I was finished with the problem, they told me that I did it wrong. Completely wrong.

I felt super stupid and embarrassed. I told them, "Yeah, okay. I'll leave now." But as I was walking to my car, I did the problem in my head. And I thought, "No, I was right!"

When I got into my car, I even got out a piece of paper and I did the problem again and thought,

The whole time I was so bummed out. Even though I was right, I still blew that interview. They weren't going to hire me.

But then that night I got a phone call from the community college people. They told me, "Hey, so we were talking about that problem with some of the calculus teachers and they all agreed that the problem had some *elements* of calculus."

Which led me to believe that these three people interviewing me for a math position really *didn't* know what a derivative was. They told me that they'd give me a second chance to teach another problem.

I was ecstatic—even though I had to go to Target to buy another polo shirt because I only owned one nice shirt, and it would be weird if I showed up in the same shirt.

When I arrived at the next interview, I got a problem about a farmer and his fence. I totally nailed it. I knew exactly how much fence that farmer needed to build two pens with one being 2x plus 3 units larger. His farm animals were going to be so happy.

The whole time I kept asking the interviewers, "Do you understand?"

And they said, "Yeah."

I thought I was doing well. I left feeling a lot more confident.

But then they never called me back.

So I didn't get the job, even though I bought a nice shirt from Target. And I kept working at Sooubway.

This is what I think: The community college people were just embarrassed that they'd given me a calculus problem, and then I totally got it right in front of them. They probably thought it would have been awkward if we worked together. That's definitely what happened. It wasn't because I actually got the problem wrong or I was a freshman and all the other tutors were in their mid-twenties. The point is, I'm not going to be teaching math anytime soon.

Still, I think interviews build character. People have told me stories about how they went to only one interview and got the job. Those people have missed out on a lot of character development. Sometimes you need to fail in life. Because you're not that special. Besides, failure makes for good stories.

Chapter 13

Things I Do That Adults Probably Don't Do

Once you turn eighteen years old, you technically cross the threshold into adulthood. You are legally and socially more responsible the second you stop being seventeen.

Now, when I turned eighteen, I didn't feel any sort of change. The planets didn't align and fulfill some prophecy.

Nope, I still woke up the same way, felt the same, and had the same likes and dislikes.

But people told me,

I was still pretty immature and didn't have the mind-set of an adult. Just look at my old YouTube videos. The very first video I posted was made by a legal adult, and he didn't know anything about recording good audio or drawing pictures in the right ratio for YouTube (1,920 pixels wide and 1,080 pixels tall, if anyone was wondering). Heck, there are kids younger than me who are more artistically talented.

Me right now

Some 14-year-old

Kasey Uhter @grgikau

Luckily, when I was first starting out, I didn't show my face in any videos, because I had a pretty awesome bowl cut.

You can tell how cool I was by the holes in my jeans. See rule #2.

Back when I legally became an adult, I did some things that I don't think people who call themselves adults do.

Actually, no—I still do these things. I started doing them when I was little and I never grew out of them. I don't know if I ever will. These things are a little embarrassing to admit, so don't make fun of me.

I'm just kidding; you probably should make fun of me for doing this stuff so that I'll stop doing it.

The first thing I do that real adults probably don't do is that I close my closet door before I sleep.

You know, because that's where monsters live. And everyone knows that monsters can't open doors—duh—so closing the closet door is a 100 percent surefire way to prevent monster attacks. If for some reason I forget to close the door, then hiding under my blanket will do the trick.

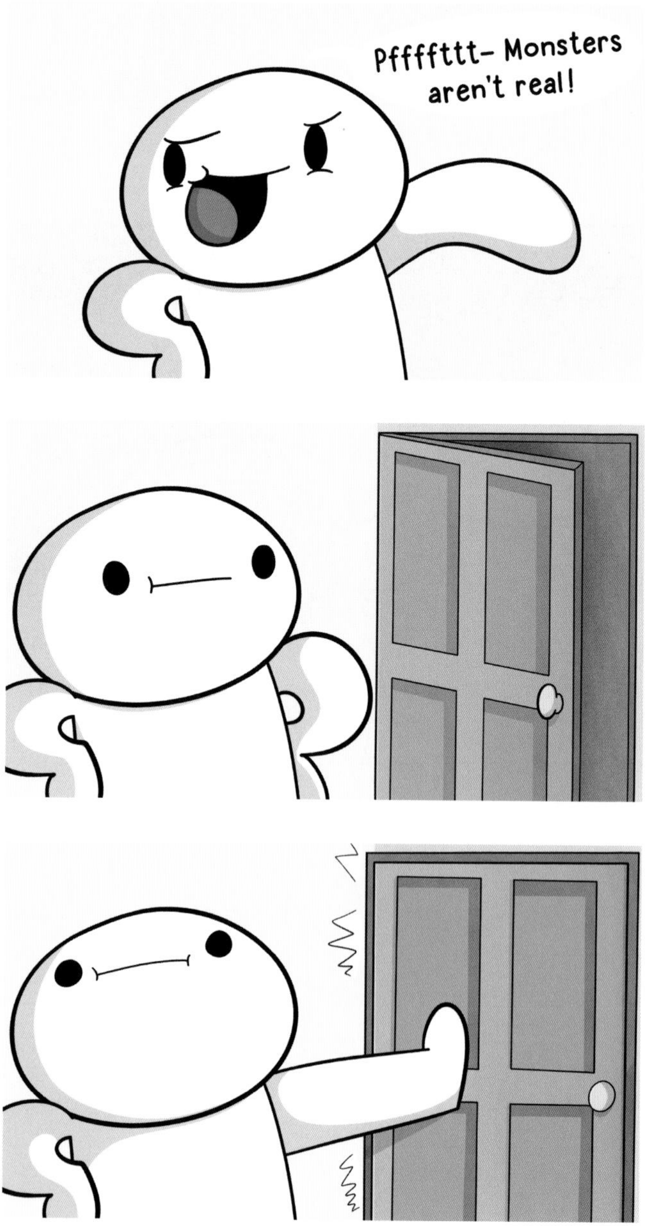
Pffffttt- Monsters aren't real!

I can't tell you why I like sleeping with my closet door closed. When I'm lying in bed and my eyes are completely shut, I can still sense whether my door is open. It's my Monster Radar. Maybe it's because it's darker than the rest of my room or because the clothes make weird shapes, but I have to close that door before I sleep.

This might happen to me when I have children.

Weirdly, during the daytime, the closet seems fine. In fact, I used to record audio for my YouTube videos in there. I've sat in that closet for an hour at a time and a monster has never appeared and attacked me. My closet isn't even that big. I sit down in it and my legs touch the walls. So if a monster was going to live in there, it would have to be really small or really skinny.

It's a weird and childish habit, I know. But I just want *you* to know, if you sleep with the closet door closed, you're not alone.

The monsters are there too.

Another thing I'm still afraid of is crossing the street. I blame my mom for instilling this fear in me. When I was little, she told me that when people drive cars, they can't see kids at all. (My mom disputes this claim.) So I always assumed that I was invisible to cars, and if I was in the street, the car wouldn't stop or slow down for me because, as my mom said, they couldn't see me.

I think this is a good way to teach kids to be afraid of cars, as they should be. The thing is that even as an adult, when I have the right of way to cross the street, I'm still on the lookout for runaway cars.

In high school, there was a road that kids had to cross to get to the school. It wasn't a busy road, mind you, only two lanes of traffic, but every now and then a car would drive by, using the road for its intended purpose.

Some kids would just walk across the road while a car was driving toward them. They were just rolling the dice, hoping that the driver was paying attention.

I don't understand what was going through these kids' minds. First of all, they were jaywalking, so they shouldn't even have been there. Second, if there's a car coming toward you, is it really smart to walk in front of it? I think it's obvious who would win in that fight.

For me, whenever I walk up to a road, my initial reaction is to look both ways. Even in the middle of nowhere. And no matter how many cars are on the road, I will always speed-walk or jog across the street.

Nowhere is safe from cars, okay? Why do we even drive them?

Another thing I do as an adult—and this is pretty embarrassing—is that I watch Minecraft videos even though I don't play Minecraft.

I had a friend ask if it was weird that he still played Minecraft and I told him yes. But for some reason, I think it's okay to *watch* someone play the game and not even play it myself. I own the game, by the way. I have an account. But I haven't really played in years.

When I first started drawing comics for the internet, I watched some TV shows (anime) or listened to music while I drew. But if I didn't feel like doing those things, I watched people play Minecraft on YouTube. There was one specific channel that I liked watching and I still like it to this day: CaptainSparklez.

I'll be watching

until the day one of us dies. (Hopefully, he's first.) I just enjoy watching other people play video games. Or maybe it's

CaptainSparklez's soothing voice. I don't know. (Sorry if you're reading this, Jordan.) But I feel like real adults get their enjoyment from watching serious stuff, like the news or something.

Another thing I do is I talk for my pets. Not *to* them like normal adults—*for* them. Not the usual, "What you got there, bud?" I'll ask them a question and then respond for them.

Each pet has a different voice and personality, which I give them.

I've been told by fans that it's not *that* weird to talk for your pets, and I've been assured that other people do the same thing, but I don't think they understand. I have conversations with these animals. I'll start talking in my normal voice, and then I'll respond to myself in either an extremely high-pitched or low-pitched voice—sometimes a Russian accent (depending on which animal is talking)—and that second voice is supposed to be what my animals would say if they could talk.

The dogs have no idea what's going on. They just hear me switching between voices every few seconds.

And to make this worse, the dogs are pretty mean to me in these conversations.

YOU SUCK!

I've built these characters and personalities around my dogs that aren't reflective of how they actually act. My dogs have "told" me to shut up. They've called me names and when I hug them they go "Ew!" But I still love them!

There's probably something psychological going on with all of this. Like deep down I secretly agree with what the dogs are saying. Either that or I'm a sociopath.

And the last thing that I do that most adults don't is: I dropped out of college to make YouTube videos.

For a while it sounded bad when people—usually really old adults, like my friends' parents—asked, "So are you going to school?"

And I had to tell them, "Nope, I dropped out and moved back in with my parents to work on my YouTube channel."

But I'm doing what I love doing, and that's drawing. I always said that I would hate getting a desk job, but now look at me—I have a job where I'm . . . sitting behind my desk all day.

Even though I'm stuck behind a desk, that doesn't mean you shouldn't still follow your dreams. Go ahead and do that. Maybe you'll get lucky.

When I was in high school making comics, it took me days to finish a comic strip. To set a goal for myself, I put this reminder above my desk:

One day, I'm not sure when, but it was probably when I hadn't done my chores, my mother made her own commentary:

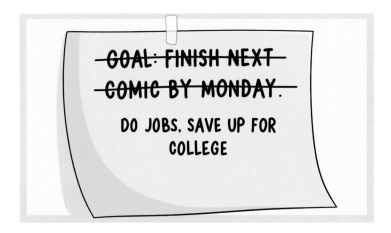

Then my older sister, I'm not sure when, but it was probably a time when she was mad at my mom, crossed that out and wrote:

I'd just been trying to remind myself to finish my comics and not cause a family philosophical debate. The thing is, both my mother and my sister had a valid point. I give a lot of tongue-in-cheek advice, but my honest advice after all of this is to follow your dreams, but do it in a smart way. Aim big, but have a backup plan. Take risks, but don't risk your life savings.

Don't listen to the haters. You can achieve great things if you work hard enough.

And remember, whatever you do in life, wear your seatbelt.

Acknowledgments

Thanks to Jordan Miller (RushLight Invader), Pantsless-Pajamas, and Vopse for helping me color the illustrations. Without them, this book—and this world—would be a lot less colorful.

Thanks to L. Harrell (Lorenmakesart) and my twin sister, Faith, for beta reading the manuscript. Without them, this book would be filled with incoherent ramblings and typos.

And a big thanks to my older sister, who bought me my first drawing tablet for my sixteenth birthday.

Thanks to my agent Tim Travaglini for using gentle persuasion and outright nagging to convince me to write this book.

Thanks to Amanda Shih, Lauren Appleton, and all of the people at TarcherPerigee who've waited patiently for me to finish.

Thanks to my family for being the source of fun times, inspiration, and an assortment of injuries.

And, of course, a big thanks to all my fans who give me the opportunity to do what I love: draw cartoons, tell stories, and occasionally make fun of corporations who will now never sponsor me.

About the Author

JAMES RALLISON has been drawing comics since he was eight years old. At age sixteen, he created the webcomic *The Odd Is Out*, which now comprises more than three hundred comics and has expanded into a YouTube channel with millions of subscribers. James lives in Arizona.